GOLF 2 TANGO 4:

The Journey of an American GI

Dale H. Petersen

Destinée SA

Published by Destinée S.A., www.destinee.ch

Cover design by Matt Deffenbaugh

ISBN 978-0-9759082-7-3

FOR DONNA
and
Amie, Nathan, and Melissa

ACKNOWLEDGEMENTS

First of all I am deeply indebted to fellow members of Company B, 159th Battalion, 101st Airborne Division (Airmobile) with whom I was privileged to serve in Vietnam in 1969 and 1970. It simply would have been impossible for me to have gotten through that year without their support, camaraderie, and friendship.

Katie Peckham had an integral role in the development and completion of my manuscript. Katie took my rough draft and spent many hours correcting grammar, improving sentence and paragraph structure and placement, and making it a much more coherent document. In addition, she pointed out many situations where I was assuming too much and needed to explain more fully military, historical, and cultural concepts. One of the most difficult things for me was her constant questioning along these lines: "What were you feeling when this happened?" "How did that affect you?" Answering those kinds of questions in my manuscript caused me to do some of the deepest searching of my soul that I've ever had to do, but in the end I found the struggle to have been very much a rewarding experience. While Katie is second to none as an editor, her greatest qualities are her gentleness, kindness, and her gifts as an encourager. She made this experience of writing a lasting joy for me.

A special thanks to Matt Deffenbaugh for designing the book's cover. I've had the privilege to enjoy Matt's artistic gifts over several years, and I feel very honored to have him give of himself for me in this way.

To my siblings and friends, thanks for your interest in my writing and your encouraging words. That has meant a lot to me.

Amie and Matt, Nathan and Michelle, and Melissa and Mark, thanks so much for encouraging me first to do this project, and then to stick with it. To my grandchildren, you may not know this now, but you also were one of my primary inspirations for writing this book. May it give you increased understanding of the history of this era and my journey through it. All of you know this already, but I'll say it again: I love you guys.

And Donna, where would I be without you? Thank you for your continuing support in this endeavor. Thanks for being there every day, on the good days of writing and the bad. You gave me time, and you gave me space. But much more importantly, you gave me your love, as you have over our past 36+ years together.

GOLF 2 TANGO 4:

The Journey of an American GI

PREFACE

As long as I can remember I wanted to fly. It never really mattered what kind of aircraft it was, I just wanted to pilot anything that could break with the ground through its own power and soar into the sky.

By the time I was nineteen years old the desire to fly had become so intense that I was ready to take concrete steps and make it a reality. Of course, the fact that I was a college sophomore who (a) didn't know what I wanted for a major, (b) wasn't doing very well in some of my classes, and (c) had no clue what I wanted to do with my life after college were probably significant motivators for me to look into flying. It soon became evident that the military provided the best avenue for learning to fly, and the pragmatic reason for this was cost — taking flying lessons on my own would require many dollars (of which I had few), whereas the military would not only give me lessons and lots of flying time for free, they'd also pay me a salary.

As I researched military flying, however, a huge roadblock presented itself — if I wanted to fly for the Air Force, Navy, Marines, or Coast Guard, I had to be a college graduate, and college was just the thing from which I wanted to get away. From my nineteen-year old perspective, graduating from college seemed inconceivable and much too arduous to pursue anyway. But then I happened onto something called the warrant officer flight training program with the Army. I didn't

1

know what a warrant officer was and didn't really care. The operative words were "flight training," and the program didn't require candidates to be a college graduate. If I made it to flight school I'd be trained to fly helicopters.

Suffice it to say I passed flight aptitude testing and an interview, and made it through Army boot camp. Then I spent virtually a year in flight school and came out with my wings and a successful transition into CH-47 Chinook helicopters. That brought me to the place where my story begins—my first assignment after flight school was to a war zone called Vietnam.

Writing the story of my year in Vietnam thirty-seven years after the fact presented some challenges. I remembered some of the days and incidents of 1969-1970 as if they'd happened yesterday. But more often than not there was a certain haziness to my memories—in some cases so faded that the memory was almost impossible to recall. Then there was the issue of looking back through the lens of all the experiences I've had since I was in Vietnam, which color the memories of that year. This made it especially difficult to discern my spiritual standpoint at the time of Vietnam, considering the thirty-seven years of increasing spiritual maturation I've undergone. I'm quite sure that what appears here of my younger self's spiritual stance is not without some of this added perspective.

If my own memories were all I had to go on to write my story, I don't think I would have stayed with the task very long at all. But I had much more to go on thanks to Donna, a key actor in my narrative. A few years ago when I first started thinking about doing this project, she said, "Oh, by the way, I kept all the letters you wrote me from Vietnam. They are in a box under the bed downstairs." Those letters turned out to be the key in getting my account written. First of all, they provided a framework of dates, places, people, etc. for my story. They also helped me recall incidents, and even jogged my memory of other situations I didn't write about in my letters but which ultimately contributed to the narrative. And occasionally I used my letters to express some of my deepest feelings about things which were transpiring in my life at the time.

I quoted from my letters quite liberally throughout my writing. I especially used direct quotes when I wrote of my feelings since I thought doing so would provide the greatest possible authenticity.

In spite of having my letters, I still had to rely heavily on my memories, which introduced the above noted concerns about their trustworthiness. As a result I know I have made mistakes. I tried my best to minimize them, but I have no doubt the mistakes are there.

I'm not very proud of some things within this account. I tried to be as honest as possible about what I wrote, but doing so was quite painful at times.

In the end this is my memoir, a story of my personal experience as best I remember it.

Chapter 1

*For the thing which I greatly feared
is come upon me,
and that which I was afraid of is come
unto me.*

--Job 3:25 (KJV)

administration buildings, and the like. And a lot of sandbagged bunkers. In fact, it seemed that there were sandbags everywhere. Dotted here and there were small semicircular pieces of corrugated metal mounted on posts about waist-high, which seemed to partially surround a hole in the ground. After a bit of puzzling, I figured out that these mysterious structures were outdoor urinals with a tiny bit of privacy—thanks to the corrugated metal.

The buses took us a few short miles to Long Binh, a huge, sprawling Army post, for initial in-country processing and unit assignments. Along the way, I saw a little of the civilian communities. Their living conditions were terribly squalid and crowded. I could see traces of what I assumed had been the French influence from the colonial days. It seemed like it had been a beautiful place a number of years ago, but the appearance was very dilapidated when I was passing by.

It wasn't long before I found out I'd been assigned to the 101st Airborne Division (Airmobile). I was very happy to find out as well that one of my best friends from flight school, Phil Lanza, got the same assignment. With everything being so new, so foreign, and with the danger of a war zone, I had been feeling quite lonely and somewhat frightened. Knowing that I would go through this with a buddy seemed to make a huge difference, like I was being thrown some sort of a lifeline.

It wasn't long before we were being bussed back to Bien Hoa where the 101st had its rear headquarters for processing replacement personnel. We would be spending about a week there, going through in-country orientation and division in-processing.

That evening as I settled into my bunk in the grungy temporary barracks, I tried to make sense of my new surroundings and my new life. Everything was so foreign, so different from anything I'd ever known—from the acrid smokiness in the air, to having to pee in semi-concealed outdoor urinals, and everything in between. I had a heavy sense of foreboding which I wanted to make sure I didn't reveal to anyone else. I thought about some things I had written to Donna a few days before I had left home: that the most important thing for me is to keep my faith in my dear Lord, to remain close to him... That my faith in God is something very precious... That he controls all things, and that everything that happens, happens because he has planned it that way. When my time for perfect joy in Glory comes, God will take me to himself whether it's by death on a sickbed, on the highways, or in a combat zone. If it is God's will, I will be protected from all things.

But then why was I feeling this fear? I had been quite relaxed at home a few days before I left. I supposed—or at least I hoped—everyone experienced some fear when they first got over here. The important thing was that I didn't want to let this fear interfere with doing my job. That's the thing that had me the most worried—that I not be a coward, that I be able to do my job the way I was supposed to.

I was drifting off to sleep when, *BOOM!* My heart felt like it had exploded in my chest, my whole body was so tensed that my muscles hurt, and sweat seemed to be coming out of every pore. Then someone said in the dark: "It's outgoing."

I relaxed just a little but my breathing was still shallow and my body was shaking. Another voice stated the obvious: "Man, that artillery battery is close."

I tried to relax a bit more, but just then an F-105 jet fighter hit his afterburners and roared down Bien Hoa's main runway, about a hundred yards from our barracks, and took off into the night sky. That ear-shattering sound was louder than the artillery.

I tried to reassure myself that the artillery and the jet were friendlies, but my body was still shaking. Even with Phil there, I was feeling very alone and scared. This was so different from Sumas. I wanted to be home, to be in the loving presence of my parents and siblings. But I was in Vietnam, and there was nothing I could do about it. As I lay there, I couldn't shake this question: *God, are you even here with me?*

*　　*　　*

Platte, South Dakota
circa 1962

It was hot before the sun had even risen. Last night I had pulled my bed back a couple feet until it was even with the open window. I had switched my pillow to the foot of my bed so I could lay my head on the window sill—anything to get a breath of cool air. Unfortunately, the air was dead, no breezes were stirring, and it was almost as hot outside as it was inside my bedroom. The only sounds outside were the chirping of the crickets and the buzzing of the cicadas. Somehow I had managed to get to sleep in spite of my discomfort, but now as a new day dawned, I had awakened to a sticky, sweaty dampness on my skin.

I knew I had to get up soon because I had told my friend Gary that I would go with him to his uncle's farm and help stack hay—I was hoping we'd get paid more than just a couple dollars.

As I slowly ate some Cheerios, I asked Dad if he had heard the weather forecast.

"I think it's supposed to be in the upper nineties again and maybe some late afternoon thunderstorms. Maybe a severe thunderstorm watch."

Oh great, I thought. *Wish we could get the rain without having the heat.*

I rode my bike to Gary's; his mom would take us to the farm a few miles south of town. As we rattled along the gravel road, we talked about how hot it was already.

"You boys be careful not to get too sunburned today," said Mrs. De Jong. We already had good tans, so I didn't think we would have a problem.

Gary's uncle already had the buckloader mounted on the Massey-Ferguson tractor. We rode on the tractor with him out to the field where we would be working.

The South Dakota prairie rolled on into the distance as far as my eyes could see. Sky and land met at the horizon at a point which seemed so far away that I would never be able to get to it. I'd heard that Montana was called the Big Sky country. I didn't think it could get any bigger than this.

I could see the hay laying neatly in windrows where it had been raked after being cut a few days ago. It was now dry enough to stack. The metal stack frame — a three dimensional rectangle made of metal bars, several feet long on each side and at least double my height — was already in place waiting to form our first haystack.

Gary and I took off our shirts, grabbed pitchforks, and went inside the frame. His uncle dropped several buck-loads of hay inside the frame, and we spread it out as he did so. As the stack grew higher, it became even more important that we do a good job of making sure there were no holes in the stack, especially by the edges of the frame. Our job was essentially a continuous process of pitching fork loads of hay and stomping it down to compact it evenly.

The sun beat down on us as it rose higher in the sky. The chaff of the hay stuck to our sweaty backs and itched something fierce. Flies buzzed around us, landing on our bodies continuously. Then I spotted the De Jongs' pickup truck bouncing out to the field which meant Gary's aunt was bringing us something to drink and eat. The ice-cold Kool-Aid chilled me pleasantly as it found its way into my stomach. I wasn't that interested in the cookies, but then when I had one I decided they hit the spot too, as long as I could drink more of that Kool-Aid.

"It's getting kinda hot for you boys out here," Gary's aunt said.

Yeah, no kidding.

"I'll make some burgers for you for lunch."

Just as long as there's plenty to drink.

After a couple more hours of stacking hay, we got on the tractor and went back to the farmhouse for lunch. Before going into the house, we went to the stock tank and stuck our heads as far under water as we could and held our breath as long as we could. The water cooled down my whole body. A couple more dunks and I was ready for lunch.

I was glad to see that there was plenty of stuff to drink, including bottles of pop—root beer, Coke, and orange soda! We hardly ever got pop at home, just Kool-Aid, which I guess was a pretty good substitute. But there was nothing like the sweet effervescence of a soda pop. And of course there was plenty of milk. All I wanted to do was drink liquids—I wasn't much interested in burgers, which was highly unusual for me. But after drinking my fill (and then some) and belching a couple times, I dug into the burgers, which tasted as good as they always did.

On the way out to the field after lunch I noticed that more of the big, white, fluffy cumulus clouds were starting to fill the skies. Dad called them fair weather clouds, at least as long as they stayed nice and white.

They had a pleasant feel, and I often dreamt what it would be like to be able to fly among them in an airplane. I just knew it would be an exhilarating experience – after all, that's how it always was in my daydreams.

The air was stifling as the sun heated the atmosphere from high overhead. "You boys better put your t-shirts on so you don't get too sunburned," Gary's uncle cautioned.

My shirt quickly got as wet as my jeans. The feel of fabric sticking to my skin was something I wanted to get away from but couldn't. Every once in awhile the sun would go behind a cloud and provide a bit of temporary relief, but the oppressive humidity didn't change.

By late afternoon most of my energy felt like it had been sapped from my body. I had downed a lot of liquids but hadn't peed much—guess I didn't need to, what with all the sweat oozing out of my skin. The sun was spending more time behind the clouds, but I don't think the temperature came down even a degree. I noticed that some of the cumulus clouds were losing their fair weather look. They were building higher and trying to fill the vast sky while taking on a darker, more menacing appearance.

"I think we've done enough for today. I better have Mother take you boys home. Looks like we could get a storm."

The rough ride on the tractor back to the farmhouse felt good. I was hot and sticky and tired, but it felt like I had done something good that day.

13

When I got home I got a big glass of ice cubes and Kool-Aid and sat drinking it at the kitchen table. Mom wanted to know about my day so I gave her a brief sketch of it. Dad came down from his study and mentioned there was a tornado watch. "You better not waste any time on your paper route."

Oh, yeah, that. As if I could forget. I couldn't remember a time in my life when I didn't deliver newspapers. Okay, so I didn't start till I was seven years old: that still seemed like most of my life. I hated it—it was always interfering with something. Any day I was swimming at the lake, I had to come home earlier than my friends because of that stupid paper route. Any time I was playing pickup baseball with the neighbor kids, I had to cut it short. This paper route was controlling my life! Today it meant I couldn't relax with another glass of Kool-Aid while watching some cartoons. Once I was on my bike and actually delivering the papers, it never seemed too bad. But I wasn't going to tell that to Dad.

As I was finishing my route that day, I started hearing the ominous rumbling of thunder. The sky was getting considerably darker, even though there were at least three hours of daylight left. As I pedaled home, I noticed a greenish hue in the boiling clouds on the western horizon.

I rode home a little quicker than usual, and although I wouldn't admit it, I felt a sense of comfort when I rolled up to the house and caught sight of Mom, Dad and my siblings.

"Man, it looks like it'll be a fun storm." I was trying to sound brave and excited.

I had a thrill/fear relationship with thunderstorms. Being able to watch a fierce Midwestern storm from the relative safety of the porch on a summer afternoon or evening was a high time for me. At the same time, with almost every thunderstorm I was sure our house would get struck by lightning. Any hint of a possible tornado sent shivers of dread through my body. This anxiety increased by at least a factor of ten after the sun had set. The darkness seemed like a giant step into the unknown, and what little control I thought I had during the daylight seemed to evaporate at night. All I could see of a storm at night were the momentary, jagged streaks of lightning; all I could do was hold my breath and cower until the rolling, pounding explosions of thunder broke the expectant silence. I knew that for every five seconds between flash and explosive crash, the lightning was a mile away from us. I would count after I saw the lightning to determine if the storm was going away from us or bearing down on us, and how close it was getting. If the lightning and thunder arrived at the same time, I knew our house had almost certainly been struck by the lightning (although in reality it had yet to happen in my lifetime).

Dad provided his usual weather update ("We're still under a tornado watch"), and Mom supplied her familiar words of comfort ("God will take care of us").

"A watch isn't as bad as a warning, is it?" someone asked hopefully.

"No, a watch means there could be a tornado, while a warning means a funnel cloud has already been spotted," said Dad as we had our weather education reviewed for the umpteenth time. "We are under a severe thunderstorm warning, though."

"Okay, everyone, it's time to eat. Wash your hands and sit down at the table," said Mom.

As everyone sat down, we bowed our heads for Dad's invocation of God's blessing on the food. I correctly guessed the following part of his prayer: "...Lord, we pray that thou wilt provide thy safety from the storm..."

The typical chaos of eight kids and two adults around our kitchen table had barely begun when the storm hit. We could hear the old house creak as a blast of wind hit. The elm trees in the backyard bent as the howling gale ripped through the branches and leaves. The lightning seemed to flash continuously, as did the rolling reverberations of thunder. The rain came down in slanting sheets, and hailstones rattled on the siding, on the windows and on the ground. Dad got up to look out the kitchen window at the storm. We eyed the door leading to the basement and the storm cellar, but no one made a move toward it. Soon several of us were at the windows, seeing and feeling the tremendous power unleashed from the heavens, experiencing the awesome, fearsome spectacle of this thunderstorm.

But the tension broke as we were jolted back to the reality of supper by a familiar voice: "Okay, you kids, get back to the table!"

In a few minutes it was over. Some hailstones, twigs, and leaves littered the ground outside. There were a few puddles of water. We could still hear some rumbling thunder receding in the distance. Dad opened the windows and back door, letting in a cool breeze. The house had not been struck by lightning. There would be no tornado on this day.

Mom always said the prayer after the meal and after Dad had read a passage from the Bible: "Dear God, we thank thee that thou didst protect us from the storm..."

Chapter 2

Since no man knows the future,
who can tell him what is to come?

--Ecclesiastes 8:7 (NIV)

4 August 1969

I had been "in-country" for less than two weeks, and I already knew my DEROS (date of estimated return from overseas) — 24 July 1970. Everyone knew his DEROS: just remember the date you left "the world" (i.e., the States) and add one year minus a day. More importantly, everyone knew the number of days he had left in country before arriving at his DEROS. I had just 354 days, or fifty-plus weeks, or 11½+ months to go, take your pick. It sounded like forever. I'd gone these two weeks without any mail. It would be awhile before I got any, since I still didn't know my exact unit assignment and therefore couldn't let anyone know my address. I was just dying for a letter; I had gone those ten days in country without anything from loved ones. I don't think anyone who has never been in the service realizes how much mail means to someone who is in the military. This need to hear from home, friends, and loved ones is even more acute when one is far away in a combat zone like Vietnam. About the only thing we had to live on was mail.

We had just completed a five-day course called P-training (P = preparatory). It was mandatory for all personnel assigned to the 101st. P-training was a lot like basic training — marching out to rifle ranges, running combat assault courses, going through ambush and booby trap training, etc. Our instructors had all been grunts and had several months' experience in "the bush" (basically anywhere on the ground outside a camp perimeter). We were also supposed to have physical training (PT) early every morning, but since it was optional for officers, I never got out of bed for it, like most of the other officers. When the enlisted troops saluted us, they were supposed to say, "All the way, sir!" Our return salute was to include the rejoinder, "Airborne!" I was having trouble getting the gung ho attitude.

Most of our instruction took place outside the perimeter fence of Bien Hoa. The first day we were out there, one of our instructors said: "If we come under fire from some bad guys out here, you all stay low and get back into the perimeter as fast as you can. We instructors will lay down covering fire until you are behind the wire."

Yeah. Okay. Man, I guess we really are in a war zone. I'm okay having these combat-experienced guys here to baby-sit us.

Almost every instructor, at some time during his presentation, would trigger an explosive charge when we least expected it. They were very loud, and we could feel the concussion. Every time that happened I was sure my heart stopped—it scared the wits out of me. I guess they wanted us to get used to detonations happening very close to us.

Several of us officers were helicopter pilots and were having trouble seeing the worth of going through P-training ourselves. I think we were just a bit arrogant.

What if we got shot down? It had been more than a year since most of us had been in boot camp, so the refresher could definitely come in handy. I suspect it was difficult for our NCO instructors, experienced combat veterans that they were, to maintain an attitude of respect for us green replacement officers, some of us who were barely out of our adolescent years.

In many ways I was still a kid, barely twenty-one years old without much life experience at all. And definitely no combat experience. I was a WO-1, a warrant officer. Historically it had been a somewhat obscure rank, but with the advent of the helicopter, and especially its wide-scale implementation in airmobile strategy and tactics, the Army used the rank of warrant officer to get thousands of helicopter pilots through flight school and into the active duty Army. Unlike commissioned officers, a warrant officer was not required to have a college degree, which allowed for a much broader field of candidates for flight school. I had a little over a year of college under my belt when I became a warrant officer candidate. Normally a warrant officer, unlike a commissioned officer, would not have any command responsibilities except the command of his aircraft crew. Other than that, a warrant officer had essentially the same prerogatives and privileges as a commissioned officer.

Tomorrow I would be boarding an Air Force C-130 cargo plane and heading north to I Corps, to join my unit. If a soldier needed an in-country flight somewhere, a C-

130 was usually his airliner. I was a little anxious about going to my unit but also excited, looking forward to the busyness that I hoped would make the time go faster, and also because it had been almost two months since I'd left flight school. It was time to get back into the cockpit.

Chapter 3

I would hurry to my place of shelter,
far from the tempest and storm.

--Psalm 55:8 (NIV)

6 August 1969

I'd made it to my unit. The C-130 flight from Bien Hoa the day before had taken all of 1½ hours. We'd landed in Phu Bai which is about five miles from the ancient capital of Hue and roughly fifty miles south of the Demilitarized Zone (DMZ) which separates North Vietnam from South Vietnam. I had spent most of the time since my arrival at Group and Battalion headquarters in Phu Bai getting briefings at both places. As usual there was a lot of hanging around with little to do. "I'm in the Army now. Hurry up and wait is our motto."

I was assigned to the 159th ASHB. The 101st had over four hundred helicopters on its books, but within that, the 159th was the only organization with CH-47 Chinooks: tandem-rotor, twin-engine, heavy-lift helicopters. The 159th had three companies—I would be in Bravo Company which was located at Camp Eagle, about five miles from Phu Bai. Bravo Company was known as "Varsity"—I didn't know where they got that weird name. But at least it was better than Playtex, which was Charlie Company's nickname. Only Alpha Company had a nickname truly fitting for a heavy lift helicopter unit—the Pachyderms. Each company had around sixteen Chinooks assigned to it.

When the introductions and orientations at Phu Bai were finally completed, a specialist from Bravo Company picked up replacement captain (and fellow

Chinook pilot) Dave Magers and myself, for the fifteen-minute jeep ride to Camp Eagle. Unfortunately my buddy Phil was not with us. He had gotten left behind in Bien Hoa because something had been messed up with his records. Supposedly he would be joining us in a day or two, but I had visions of him getting sent to another organization somewhere else in-country, where it would be a long time before I'd see him again.

Driving between posts was about the only chance we ever got to see the local Vietnamese communities: otherwise, everything outside post perimeters was off limits. I was fascinated by the sights of the villages we passed through. Everything seemed so crowded. Poorly constructed shanties were everywhere. Some hovels were nothing more than pallet-size cardboard boxes emblazoned with "Pentax," "Panasonic," "Budweiser" — obvious discards from a military post exchange (PX). There were several merchant stands along the road selling such things as Coke, Army canteens, cigarettes, even "C-rations," or "combat rations," consisting of a few cans of food and a pack of four cigarettes in a small cardboard box. Interesting to think of how they might have gotten all that stuff.

The people came in all ages. Every once in awhile we'd see rather distinguished-looking elderly men, white hair and beards neatly trimmed, white, pajama-looking outfits setting them apart from the others. I guessed they were probably well-respected in their communities, perhaps the "wise old men" of the village. The other adults wore a variety of clothing, often black pajama-style dress. There were many *mama-sans* (a designation G.I.s applied to virtually any adult Vietnamese female) of varying ages carrying on conversations wherever I looked. Some girls or young women that I figured were in their older teens or early twenties, wore full-length dresses of pink, lavender, or similar colors. Several of them were rather attractive ... until they smiled and showed off their black teeth. In fact, virtually everyone except young children, had blackened teeth.

"All the Vietnamese chew betel nut. Makes their teeth black," said our driver when we noted this. "Heard it has some kind of narcotic in it."

Soon a large, sprawling base camp came into view. My first impression was that it had once been an open, natural field until several bulldozers had gotten into it and scraped various places level on which to build the "home" of the 101st. All around the perimeter there were bunkers with firing ports looking out over rows and rows of concertina and other wire. The interior of the base looked like it held literally hundreds of slapped-together buildings and large tents—all strictly utilitarian, making no bow to aesthetics. Yet there were some green areas running through the gray-brown drabness of the place. As always, sandbags were everywhere—forming bunkers, stacked around buildings, scattered individually on building roofs.

This was Camp Eagle, home to many organizations including the 101st Division headquarters

(HQ). A number of infantry units called it home as well, when they weren't in the bush. In addition, it was the base for several helicopter companies—UH-1 Hueys, or "slicks," which were the most prevalent choppers, used primarily for carrying G.I.s and smaller supply loads; AH-1G Cobra gunships, or "snakes," basically weapons platforms with mini-guns (like a gatling gun) and 2.75-inch rockets; LOH-6 light observation helicopters, serving as airborne scouts and, at times, small weapons platforms; and, of course, Chinooks.

Once inside the perimeter, it wasn't long before Varsity's company area came into view. Our next-door neighbors were the Toros, a Cobra gunship company. That was another rather appropriate nickname for a unit (at least in comparison to "Varsity"). Our company area was situated alongside a little draw. A small creek flowed through it, and as a result we had some green grass and foliage. Spread out along either side of the creek were several revetments, parking spaces for the Chinooks designed to minimize damage from rocket or mortar attacks. Just beyond the Chinook revetments were the officer quarters, complete with a small "O" club, or "officers' club." Down a small hill from the revetments, east of the officer quarters, rose a large maintenance hangar with spaces for three Chinooks. Further down the creek from the officer quarters were the mess hall and the enlisted men's barracks. And roughly in the center of the company area we had a special luxury—a small outdoor theater (complete with screen, benches, and projection booth) which featured movies several nights a week.

When the jeep stopped in the company area, the first thing I noticed was that same putrid, smoky smell that gagged me when I arrived in-country. At least now I knew what it was. While still at Bien Hoa, someone had explained the facts of life to me regarding the disposal of human waste: "When you're in the outhouse doin' your thing, its not going into a deep hole in the ground. There's nothing there but fifty-five-gallon drums, cut in half, below you. Every day it's somebody's job to pull out those drums, put some kerosene in them, and light 'em on fire. Rather sanitary when all is said and done."

According to what I'd been told, Varsity had decent living conditions for officers in the 101st Division. They were by no means great by Stateside comparison, but I guess they proved to be relatively comfortable for in-country. There were two rows of rooms, called hootches, facing each other across a cement walkway which ran between them. Each row looked something like a very cheap single-story motel. They were primarily of plywood construction although two of the four walls had large screened window openings. There were also pieces of plywood on hinges that could be swung up over the screens in case of inclement weather. Narrow wall lockers had been modified to include a light bulb in the bottom of each one—this provided a means for counteracting the dampness and mildew that plagued every soldier's clothing. I was surprised to find that each room had electrical outlets and a sink with cold running water. Even more surprising, the communal showers had hot water—a huge luxury! Some enterprising previous tenants had rigged up water tanks with immersion heaters.

I didn't waste any time getting my first hot shower since leaving home. Afterward I unpacked my duffel bag and tried to make myself at home. I didn't have a roommate yet, but what with so many people coming and going, I figured it wouldn't be too long before I had one. I wished Phil were there.

It seemed to be real quiet in comparison to Bien Hoa where jets were constantly screaming down the nearby runway. The only noise came from a couple of nearby artillery positions which produced a loud boom every once in awhile.

It had been a long day and I was ready to hop in bed.

KAWUMP!

"INCOMING!"

I heard the sound of footsteps running down the walkway outside my door.

"Look out!" "Get out of my way!" Voices were yelling near and far.

The bunker was no more than ten running strides from my door. After a split second of hesitation—*what'll I do, risk getting run over on the sidewalk or risk getting hit by shrapnel in my room?*—I joined the crowd making a beeline for the bunker. As I got inside the sandbagged structure, I was gasping for breath and my heart was pumping wildly. *I don't get it,* I thought to myself. *It feels like I ran two miles instead of ten steps. I hope that's not fear making an appearance again.* Somehow I was feeling a little safer in the bunker than I had a few seconds before in my room.

"Sounds like mortars."

"No, we always get rockets."

"It don't matter, if we take a direct hit in here, we're all dead."

So much for my feeling safe.

There was a jumble of voices talking over each other excitedly. Soon someone started singing a song which cast a dim light on our leadership. I learned that the 101st Airborne Division Screaming Eagles were really the Puking Buzzards, at least according to my fellow soldiers. The adrenaline was flowing and everyone seemed in high spirits. I supposed they were feeling good to have made it to the bunker, despite the possibility that they would still be done in by a direct hit. Apparently, conventional wisdom maintained that the bunker was the safest place for anything but a direct hit. Our rooms had a perforated steel plate (PSP) barrier filled with sand along the outward facing walls, but that was only one side. Of course, running to the bunker when rockets or mortars were raining down had its own hazards.

I hoped this didn't happen too often because it sure could interfere with getting a good night's sleep.

One thing I wouldn't do was write to my parents about this. My poor mother worried enough the way it was, and I simply didn't want to give her any more pain. I had already planned to sanitize my letters home because of that.

At that moment, someone looked at me and said, "Hey, Petersen, welcome to Camp Eagle!"

Chapter 4

Turn to me and be gracious to me,
for I am lonely...

--Psalm 25:16 (NIV)

9 Aug 1969

Dear Donna,

Here I am on a Saturday night. At least I think it's Saturday night. After you've been here for awhile, all the days seem the same and you start to lose all track of time. The only thing I'm sure of is that I have 349 days to go. I should quit counting the days because the time seems to go too slow that way...

I'm in my first lonely, depressed mood. I guess the main reason is that I haven't been doing much the past couple days except little obnoxious-type things. I hope you don't mind if I write to you when I'm in this frame of mind...I think once I start getting some mail, it'll help a lot. I never realized that contact with the 'world' and loved-ones could be so important. I guess I was too independent in my own ways, that I figured I could function alone in my own world. No, I never really was a loner; I always had a lot of friends and associates. I guess it takes a deprivation of these things to make one realize how much relationships really mean. I don't think a person can really function as a total human being without the love and companionship of friends and loved-ones...

I think another of my problems is that all my friends from flight school went to different units. I'm in a strange environment with all strange faces. Actually, it's like this every time one goes to a new place. It takes a few days to become familiar with everything and to start to feel at home. Also, when I think about how so many people are thinking of me and praying for me (as you are doing), it makes things seem much better. Don't worry about me; I'm just in one of those

33

moods tonight. I'll get over it with no problem. Around here, it's known as a 'low morale factor'...

Oh yes, I got my graduation pictures just before I left home. I forgot to enclose one in my last letter to you, so will do it this time. Kinda dumb, isn't it. The only good thing on it is the silver wings. They are my pride and joy...

Like I said, I haven't been doing much of anything for the past couple days. I've mainly been trying to get settled in my room and get all my necessary equipment. I had to get my flight suits, armored chest protector, flak vest, pistol (that's not a water pistol), survival gear (in case I get shot down. Yipe!), gas mask, and other trash like that. I've also had a lot of material to read about the company's S.O.P. (standard operating procedures).

The reason I haven't been flying yet is because each newly assigned pilot in Vietnam has to have a check ride and an orientation ride to help familiarize him with the local flying area and the standard procedures of the unit he is assigned to. Well, it so happens that the standardization pilot of this company who gives these flights is down south on assignment. They won't let me fly until I get checked out by him. That's the rules. He should be back in a day or two so I can start flying...

Oh, I've been trying to work that Southern accent out of my speech. I don't know if I'm successful or not...

Luv, Dale

*   *   *

11 Aug 69

Dear Donna,

I had my happiest day yesterday since I left home. Remember in the letter I wrote Saturday (Aug. 9) how I told you that I had been separated from all my buddies from flight school?

...I was in my room yesterday afternoon getting some of my things organized, when Phil walked into my room! They had gotten his records straightened up, and he got assigned to the very same company I'm in! In fact, we got assigned to the same room so we're now roommates. You just can't believe how happy I was to see him. I still can't believe it's actually true, that he is actually here. I hadn't even dared hope for anything like that, but it was an answer to many prayers. It increased my morale by 100%. Besides being able to go home, that was about the best thing that could've happened to me. I just hope we'll be able to stay in the same unit for the duration of our tour.

Not only that happened yesterday, but also I got to go to a chapel service. It was the first opportunity I've had since I left home. It sure meant a lot to me. I think a person takes things like that too much for granted and doesn't realize how much it really means until he is deprived of it. Our Lord sure provides for our needs. What's really great is that the chapel is only a short walk away at our Group HQ. There is a chaplain permanently assigned to it, so that means they have regularly scheduled services there each Sunday. You don't find that too often here in Vietnam except at the larger base camps. Of course, we do fly seven days a week...

Luv, Pete

Chapter 5

*...they shall mount up with wings as
eagles...*

--Isaiah 40:31 (KJV)

Lansing, Illinois
circa 1956

Vacation time was always one of the highlights of my year. This time, we had just reached our first destination, and little did I know that one of my greatest dreams was about to come true. We were in a suburb of Chicago with my mom's relatives. I always loved going to see my Uncle Phil and his family, and Aunt Kay. I felt very welcomed and loved there. Being there always meant going to the beach on Lake Michigan, a visit to the zoo, outdoor picnics, frequent walks to the corner grocery store for ice cream, and watching TV—something we didn't have at home. Best of all, Dad would bring my older brother Don and I to a baseball game, usually at Wrigley Field where the Cubs played their home games. The thrill here was never just attending the game— getting there was half the fun. We would take a commuter train to the Chicago Loop (downtown), then an "el" (elevated train tracks through the center of the city) train to the ballpark.

And getting to Chicago from South Dakota was part of what I loved about vacation time, too, even though it was a seven-hundred-mile car ride, and meant two adults and six kids being jammed together for an all-day marathon. The night before we would leave, Dad would pack the top of the car so that we would be ready to hit the road at 4 a.m. The day of transit would see many potty stops, a morning and an afternoon stop for a treat of ice cream, and a midday stop for a picnic lunch.

Dad would use the picnic stop to hit us some pop flies (all the more to be ready for a foul ball at Wrigley Field). The best stop for me was always the one that included supper at a drive-in: hamburgers, French fries and a milk shake. I was in heaven—ice cream three times in one day. My favorite way to pass the time in the car, was to follow our progress on the map. Because of my love of maps, I had become the unofficial navigator for the family at a rather young age. After supper the excitement would build as we would approach the greater Chicago area. Farmland would turn into outlying suburbs, which in turn would lead to urban areas. Of course the car radio would be tuned to a ballgame. At around 9 p.m., we would reach our destination.

My Uncle Phil was a hero to me for a variety of reasons, but primarily because he owned and flew his own Piper Cub airplane. I was already fascinated by the concept of flying although I had never been airborne. I used to try to imagine what it would be like. When Dad would go to church meetings in Michigan, he would usually fly there. When he would come home, I'd always pump him with a thousand questions so I could vicariously experience the minutest details of flying.

Little did I know what surprise awaited me in Chicago that year – greater even than the thrill of a Cubs game with Dad and Don. After dinner that particular night in Chicago, Uncle Phil looked at my parents and asked, "Do you think it would be okay if I took Donnie and Dale up for a plane ride this evening?"

They gave their consent. I almost peed in my pants, I was so excited.

We went to the airport that very evening. I couldn't sit still in the car on the way: I was continually bouncing on the seat. When we got to the airport and the hangar, I helped Uncle Phil open the hangar door. I thought I wouldn't be able to breathe when I saw that little airplane sitting there. My brother and I were allowed to help push the plane out of the hangar. It was a magical time for me: touching the fabric of the wings, watching my uncle go though his preflight inspection, smelling the oil and fuel, and then climbing in and getting strapped into my seat.

When the engine started, I could hardly contain myself. The taxi time to the end of the runway was all a blur. Before I knew it, we were at full throttle, roaring down the grass airstrip. At age eight, few experiences in my life equaled the thrill I got the moment I left the ground for the first time. This fantasyland, in which I was actually the one viewing the earth from the air, gave me a deep sense of joy and awe.

It took me a long time to get to sleep that night, but when I did my dreams could only replay my life-changing experience of that evening. A couple days later, I would bask in the glory of being at a major league baseball game in Wrigley Field. But for the rest of the summer and beyond, it would always be that, my first airplane ride, which would be at the forefront of my mind.

*   *   *

13 August 1969

"Mr. Petersen. Sir. It's time to wake up." An insistent, loud-whispering voice finally got my attention. I was having a hard time clearing the sleepiness from my brain. As I came to consciousness, I noticed the room was still dark except for the flashlight of the operations clerk.

"You'll be flying with Mr. Reeder today on your check ride. Your aircraft's tail number is 142. It's in the revetment closest to the O Club."

I was finally going flying today—the first time in about seven weeks. I felt a little anxious and yet quite excited. I knew I'd be kind of rusty since it had been so long since I'd last flown. Also, up until this day, all my flying had been in flight school. Now for the first time all my flying would be operational. I really didn't want to screw up or make a fool of myself. Yet I was pretty sure I'd get back the feel of the aircraft quickly. At the same time, I knew I had a ton of stuff to learn—this was no longer the friendly environs of the airfield at Fort Rucker, Alabama, this was tactical flying in a war zone.

I got up and washed my face with the cold water which was piped to our sink. I put on my Nomex flight suit for the first time and headed to the mess hall to get some breakfast. There was a short line on the officers' side so it didn't take too long to get something to eat. I could hear the usual complaints about powdered eggs.

Actually I had no problems with them—to me they tasted just like the scrambled eggs they were purported to be.

"Hey, Petersen, you flying with Veryl today?"

I nodded in the affirmative.

"Don't believe everything he tells you. We do some things differently than the book says around here, but we'll orient you the right way when you start flying with us."

I quickly finished my breakfast and walked back toward my room to pick up my gear. Along the way, I saw that someone had already brought some leftovers to Gork, Varsity's pet pig. Somewhere in the not-too-distant past, a small pig had materialized from who knows where, and folks started feeding that thing morning, noon and night. It was huge the first time I saw it, the biggest sow I had ever laid eyes on. It did nothing but lie around and feast on mess hall chow. Someone had honored Gork by naming our outdoor theater after her—the name was even painted on the back of the screen.

After picking up my helmet, chicken plate (our word for the armored chest protectors we wore while flying), pistol, survival gear, and other paraphernalia, I headed out to the aircraft. The flight engineer and crew chiefs were just finishing their preflight inspection of the aircraft, during which they checked for safety related problems. They had left open the access covers, doors and fairings for the pilots' preflight inspection. I sometimes wondered about the benefit of us pilots doing a preflight check after the flight engineer and his crew chiefs had already done a more extensive preflight than we would do. But almost from day one of flight school it had been drummed into us that no pilot should ever get into an aircraft and start flying until he himself has done a preflight inspection. There were all kinds of stories about pilot preflights uncovering broken safety wire, foreign objects in critical areas, low fluid levels, and just about any other hazardous situation you could think of.

I waited until Veryl showed up and then did the preflight with him looking over my shoulder. I made sure I had my pocket-size "Pilot's Checklist for CH-47B and C Helicopters," and that I followed it religiously since Veryl was the check pilot. Veryl was a real stickler for doing things by the book. He could get quite indignant when pilots were lax about these kinds of things. I had done enough Chinook preflights during CH-47 transition training at the Fort Rucker flight school to be able to do it from memory, but today I would use the checklist since that was the official way of doing it.

We did the exterior check, looking for fluid leaks and obstructions of the numerous inlets and outlets, making certain the rotor blade tie-downs had been removed, and ensuring the integrity of myriad safety wires, among other checks. Then we climbed up on the fuselage and did the same thing on top, after which we completed the interior checklist items in the cargo compartment. The flight engineer followed us through our preflight and closed access doors and covers as we finished with them. The two crew chiefs, who also served as the door gunners, mounted their M-60 machine guns on the left- and right-hand sides respectively and finished their preflight preparations.

After the inspection was complete, I settled into the right pilot's seat and put on my seat belt and shoulder harness, and adjusted the seat and pedals. Butterflies took over my gut as the familiar sights and smells of the cockpit invaded my senses, and a shiver coursed through my body in anticipation of being airborne in a few short minutes. I inserted my earplugs, pulled on my helmet, plugged my communications cord into the aircraft receptacle, and adjusted the helmet's microphone so that it was touching my lips. Not everyone used earplugs, but I found the high-pitched scream of the forward transmission, which was located just behind and above the pilot seats, to be so noisy as to be almost painful; plus I had a hard time hearing my radios without the earplugs. Then we went through the "Before Starting Engines Check," checking lights and circuit breakers, setting switches, and various actions on the console and instrument panel. There was an armored plate on the side of the pilots' seats that had to be adjusted forward to cover our shoulders. Armored plating was also found on the bottoms and backs of our seats. I adjusted my pistol and holster until it was between my legs—that wasn't a part of the checklist, but it was a part of pilot lore that such a precaution had deflected bullets previously. I figured it was probably a fable, but then I wasn't going to tempt fate either.

"You can go ahead and start it," Veryl said over the intercom.

Man, it's finally going to happen. We 'kicked the tires' and now we're going to 'light the fire!' "Roger that. Chief, do you read me?" I asked the flight engineer in the back.

"Loud and clear, sir."

I did an intercom check with the door gunners as well.

I pressed the master caution test switch to make sure all caution panel lights were working.

"Okay, P to start."

"P to start," echoed the flight engineer from his position aft of the helicopter.

I pushed the APU-AGB switch to start, then moved the APU control switch to the start position and held it there; the familiar whine of the small turbine engine started to increase in pitch. I watched the APU tachometer rise to ninety percent, then released the APU start switch. The APU was running normally, and the caution lights had gone out as they should, so I released the APU-AGB switch. As the hydraulic systems came on line, the rotor blades flexed slightly, like a bird beginning to flap its wings prior to flight.

Now we could start our main engines. Prior to main engine start, I went through a series of checks — various gauges and systems like hydraulic and oil pressure and temperature, lights, resetting the wheel parking brakes, and flight controls' movement limits.

"Number one to start," I said over the intercom.

"Number one to start," repeated the flight engineer, letting me know he was in position to check for an engine fire during the start sequence.

I moved the engine condition lever for engine number one to "ground" (idle). Then I flipped the ignition switch to "on" and opened the "start fuel" switch for engine number one. As I depressed the start button, I could hear the turbine engine start to whine and could see the front rotor blades begin to turn. When nI speed (turbine speed in percentages) reached thirty-five percent, I closed the start fuel switch and released the start pushbutton. After a quick check of engine instruments, I said, "Number two to start."

"Number two to start," sounded in my earphones.

I went through the same process for engine number two, and soon both engines were idling normally, with rotor RPM about eighty. "Engines to flight." I advanced both engine condition levers to the flight position, and the rotor RPM quickly accelerated to 210. I used my "engine beep trim" switch to bring the rotors to normal flight operating RPM of 230. When the engines and rotor RPM were stabilized, I shut down the APU.

We went through the various checks of instruments, gauges and caution panel lights called for by our "Ground Operations Check." Veryl said, "Okay, I'll let you take off. Some of the guys do a vertical takeoff of a hundred feet or more. That's dangerous and unnecessary. I'm going to write them up one of these days." That was Veryl for you. "The right way to do it is to back out of the revetment at a normal hover, then do a normal takeoff."

"Roger that."

"Okay," Veryl went on, "I've got the UHF on the Eagle tower frequency. Our call sign is our tail number, so today we're Varsity 142. Our home station is called the Locker Room. When you're ready, request takeoff. I'll help you if you need it."

I had flipped on my UHF radio receiver switch so I had already heard a couple aircraft request and receive takeoff clearance. It sounded like a pretty standard protocol. I turned my radio transmitter dial to UHF, depressed the radio switch on my cyclic stick grip, and said: "Eagle tower, Varsity 142."

"Go ahead, Varsity."

"Varsity 142 is in the Locker Room for takeoff."

"Roger, Varsity 142. Winds are 210 [degrees, which meant that the winds were coming out of the southwest; 360 degrees would be out of the north] at seven knots. Altimeter is two niner niner eight [29.98 — barometric pressure]. You are cleared for a southwest departure."

"Roger, southwest departure." Then I depressed the intercom switch: "Clear me."

"We're clear on the left."

"Clear on the right."

"Clear in the back."

With my left hand on the thrust control lever, I provided upward pressure which increased the pitch on all the rotor blades simultaneously. At the same time, I nudged the cyclic stick backwards slightly with my right hand. The two actions caused the front wheels to come off the ground to the normal "nose-high hover" attitude of a Chinook. Then, slight pressure forward on the cyclic and more upward movement on the thrust lever, and we were free of the ground. We came up to about ten feet at a stationary hover, then with aft movement of the cyclic, we backed away from the revetment until we were over the little creek in the draw. A left pedal turn brought the aircraft around to the southwest, then with a more pronounced forward movement on the cyclic stick and upward movement on the thrust lever, the nose of the helicopter dipped and airspeed and altitude increased rapidly. We accelerated to about eighty knots and increased altitude at around five hundred feet per minute, for a normal climb.

Once again I experienced the thrill of being free of the ground. Opening up before me was that whole new world, in which objects on the ground diminished in size, new horizons began to spread out before me, and I climbed into the vastness of air and space and sky. Being in the air gave me such a feeling of freedom, of exhilaration. I was almost like a little kid who had gotten a new toy. I continued with my regular checks of gauges and instruments, keeping a lookout for other aircraft and communicating perfunctorily on the radios and

47

intercom—all the normal flying activities. But inside of me, my spirit was soaring. And I smiled.

Chapter 6

...He makes the clouds his chariot
and rides on the wings of the wind...
How many are your works, O Lord!
In wisdom you made them all...

--Psalm 104:3, 24 (NIV)

16 August 1969

I checked the pool table in the O Club. A lot of mail there, but still none for me. The mail clerk put all the officers' mail there, and I'd been checking it daily since I arrived. I figured I would have something by now because I'd written Donna and my folks the day I arrived at Varsity and found out my mailing address. The central thought in my mind was: "I've just gotta hear something from someone really soon."

One good thing was that I'd been flying missions since my successful check ride. As I'd expected, I was a little rusty at first because of the long layoff since flight school. My ACs helped me along at first, and after awhile I felt right at home again in the cockpit. The AC was the aircraft commander, or head pilot— the "man-in-charge" of the aircraft. The other pilot (me) was known as just the pilot. I was scheduled with the more experienced ACs at first—for my benefit as well as the whole company's benefit.

It took two pilots to fly a helicopter in a tactical environment because of the heavy workload — navigating, operating the radios, making various systems checks—in addition to the actual flying itself. One of the most important functions of the non-flying pilot was to operate the engine beep trim switch, or simply "the beep," during a load pickup. The beep is a switch that controls the power settings of the engines and therefore the rotor RPM. When picking up an eight-thousand-pound load (roughly the average load that we carried), it took most of the power of the Chinook's engines. Because of that, there was a tendency to lose some rotor RPM as the load was lifted off the ground, a potentially dangerous situation. By using the beep switch, we were able to add power to the engines and maintain rotor RPM during that critical flight maneuver.

We usually split up the different jobs, although more often than not the AC did a bit less of the actual flying and a bit more of the other tasks.

Our AO, or "area of operation," was in I Corps, the northernmost part of South Vietnam, and it included just about everything from Danang in the south up to the DMZ in the north, and from the Pacific Ocean on the east to Laos in the west. The countryside was quite interesting—so different from home—and had a real beauty to it. In the east the deep turquoise waters of the South China Sea sparkled to the horizon. Miles and miles of white sandy beaches stretched from north to south as far as the eye could see. Inland, the primary color turned to the emerald green of ubiquitous rice paddies on the flat coastal plain. Winding rivers and quaint little villages with grass huts were scattered among the rice paddies. A few larger villages appeared quite run-down, but there were traces of what I guessed were French influences from a prior era, and it seemed like this had been quite a prosperous area before the war.

We regularly flew over the city of Hue, the ancient imperial capital of Vietnam. A large portion of the city was called the Citadel of Hue and was surrounded by a mostly intact ancient wall. There were some beautiful temples, Buddhist statuary and historical buildings in the Citadel. The Perfume River wound its way through the city. There were still a lot of battle scars from the Tet offensive of 1968 when the Vietcong had overrun the city and holed up in the Citadel for three weeks before being driven out.

More of our flying was done to the west, in the mountains, than along the coastal plain. Those ominous-looking mountains towered above the flatlands, up to six thousand feet and more. They reminded me a lot of Washington, where the Cascades reached heavenward from the coast near my home. The mountains were rugged and spectacular, although they also bore many scars of the war. Bomb craters dotted the steep terrain and valleys. Dense jungle with trees over two hundred feet high had been stripped of their foliage in places by chemical defoliants. This gave the bad guys less of a place to hide, although much of the terrain still hid thousands of them.

Most of our missions were in support of remote firebases, so called because they provided artillery support for infantry field units. These firebases were usually on mountaintops or narrow ridges which had been bulldozed to provide a level area big enough to hold a battery of six 105-mm or four 155-mm artillery guns. Sometimes these firebases could be located in valleys as well. Our Chinooks had brought the engineers and bulldozers to these locations to make the firebases in the first place. The kinds of supplies we would carry to these locations were almost anything the "cannon cockers" (artillery personnel) needed in order to live and accomplish their mission, especially artillery rounds, small weapons ammo, large rubberized containers for water and fuel, C-rations, and mail. Almost all our loads were carried externally by slings attached to the cargo hook on the underside of the helicopter.

By this time I was getting used to a weekly occurrence which I found to be decidedly unpleasant— taking anti-malarial pills. We'd been warned since boot camp not to skip this important treatment because many G.I.s died as a result of ignoring the medication and subsequently contracting malaria. I had no problems with the daily little white pills. It was the big orange pill we took once a week which seemed to turn my intestines inside out. I had to make sure I was close to an outhouse for a couple hours after downing that weekly scourge.

Chapter 7

*[The Lord] satisfies your desires with
good things
so that your youth is renewed like the
eagle's.*

--Psalm 103:5 (NIV)

17 August 1969

I couldn't believe it! There was mail with my name on it! There was news from the world! I carefully checked all the mail on the pool table to make sure I had all that belonged to me. There was the familiar typewritten envelope with my home address in Washington—a letter from my Dad who was the primary letter-writer of our family. And there were THREE, count 'em—THREE, from Donna.

I wasn't about to dash through those letters. I wanted to savor them in a quiet place, so I brought them to my hootch. There was a painful joy in reading Dad's letter. It was typical of most of his letters: a short synopsis of the goings and comings of the family, reaction to my previous letters, weather, and sports. The familiar rhythms of my family's life infused my soul, and I smiled as I felt the comforting vibrations fill my being. Yet it was an experience from a distance, from the outside looking in, so in reality it was not a family experience at all. While I smiled, I couldn't stop the tears, and I was glad there was no one else in the room with me.

Donna's letters were beautiful, but I didn't quite know what to make of our relationship. We hadn't known each other long at all. I had met her in church on a visit to the Detroit area to see my sister and her husband while I was still in flight school. While on leave after flight school, I had taken a detour back to Detroit on my way home. We'd spent part of a couple days together and really hit it off. I guessed that at least part of her reasoning for writing me was to do her patriotic duty. But we had also talked about using correspondence as a way to get to know each other better during my year's tour in Vietnam.

I was quite taken with Donna. She was a very attractive young woman, both in her physical beauty and her inner character. She seemed very mature for her age. Yet I knew there was no way we should even be considering any kind of a commitment to each other for quite awhile because of how little time we'd spent together and how little we knew each other. If the truth be told, I was wary of getting burned, which had happened before and was not a pleasant experience. At the same time, I definitely wanted to continue getting to know her better. And that was the only commitment we really had—to learn what we could about each other for a year through correspondence, and then see what happened when I got back to the world and we could spend time together. It was good for me to have someone to share my feelings and experiences with, because there were a lot of things about which I didn't want to worry my parents.

I figured I had lingered long enough with my mail. I needed to get some work done before heading for the chow hall for some dinner. I had been given a secondary duty as a finance officer. So far it was nothing more than converting Vietnamese *piasters* and MPC, or military payment certificates. The MPC seemed like funny money, but we weren't allowed to have greenbacks in country, so that's all we had to spend. I don't think the powers-that-be wanted black market currency transactions done with greenbacks because that could get out of hand in a hurry. But everything I'd heard told me there was plenty of black market trading done with MPC.

I hoped there was a good movie that night. Of course, I would almost certainly be at Gork Theater tonight, regardless of what it was.

Later that night at about 10 p.m., just before I hopped in bed, I heard a distant "kawump!" and sirens going off at about the same time. I had learned to distinguish incoming and outgoing very quickly. The incoming had sort of a two "syllable" sound while the outgoing just had a single BOOM. As usual I made a quick beeline for the bunker. We didn't hear any close impacts, so the rockets probably landed somewhere else in Camp Eagle or outside the perimeter.

At 2 a.m. I was again rudely interrupted out of a deep sleep by the eerie wailings of the sirens. I surprised myself at how quickly I could wake up and run to the bunker. That was not a formula for a good night's sleep, though.

Chapter 8

*And we know that in all things God works
for the good of those who love him...*

--Romans 8:28 (NIV)

18 Aug 69

Dear Donna,

...You asked about the attitudes of guys over here. That's a rather tough question, but I'll do what I can with it. Most of them here have one foremost thought in their minds — going home. I think a lot of them appreciate it when someone tells them sincerely that they are proud of the jobs they are doing, and they (the people in the US) feel indebted to them (us over here). Sincere remarks of backing like this aren't too prevalent, though. I don't think too many are exactly overjoyed at the fate of being here. But I'm sure that when they finally do get home, they have a deep sense of pride of having done something their country has asked, of having been here and accomplishing a mission. I have many deep, complicated feelings of my own about the whole situation here, but it would take a book to explain them all...

Not a whole lot has been happening around here. The lull in the war continues. There are scattered firefights and mortar and rocket attacks, but no big offensives or operations. Either Charlie Cong is preparing for a big, all-out push, or is in a general de-escalation because he is badly hurt after years of fighting. It's anybody's guess. And so the war goes on.

Last night the enemy (Chuck or Charlie as he is known here) launched two different rocket attacks on our Camp Eagle. Most of the rockets fell outside the perimeter, and very little damage was done. I just hope ol' Chuck doesn't get more accurate...

Love, Pete

*   *   *

59

23 Aug 69

Dear Donna,

...*I love your letters. It's just the kind of things I like to hear: what you're doing, what you like to do, how you feel about certain things, the questions you have, or just good old "jabbering," as you call it. I just love it. It makes things seem so bright, happy, fresh, alive: just the sort of things I need to hear...*

It was good to read about your thoughts and relationship to God. Yes, we do both "think, pray to, and get answers from the same God," as you so beautifully put it. Things do seem so wonderfully different, and experiences so much more meaningful when our Lord is in the middle of all things. We must remember, and be given the assurance, that all things that happen in our lives – good or bad – have a purpose. Our Lord works out all these things – whether they seem good or bad to us – for our own good. I have that peace, even about being here and the things that could happen if they were God's will.

You asked me how Sundays are over here. Well, I've lost almost all sense of time...Days and weeks all seem the same...I did get to chapel the past two Sundays, but that was the only distinguishing thing about it...

Today is the first day I haven't had to fly this week. It sure felt good to sleep in once. That means I'll be flying tomorrow, though, so I won't be able to go to chapel. Tonight we're having a cookout, something we have every Sat. evening. (The luxuries we have around here!) We usually have steaks, chicken, ribs, hamburgers, or anything else we can "requisition." We barbecue them over a big grill which we *made by cutting 55 gal. drums in half. It's a pretty effective barbecue pit! Tonight, we also get an added extra special thing: a U.S.O. show! It's a rock group from the States. I'm getting all excited about it. Any entertainment that reminds us of home is <u>great</u>. It's gonna be great to hear the pounding of the drums, the throbbing sounds of the bass, the pulsating rhythms of guitars. We're gonna really groove out tonight.*

Guess who I saw this past Thurs.? Miss America! No kidding, either. I guess her and some others who were runners-up in the pageant were making the rounds, seeing all the good, li'l troopies. It was noon, and most of us were noisily slopping chow in the mess hall (That's a crude way of saying we were eating.). Well, in she walks and everyone quiets down. Everyone quit eating and commenced to drooling and foaming at the mouth. Course, I didn't; she didn't phase me in the least. (??) (Ha, Ha!) They just came around and chatted with us for awhile...

You asked about newspapers. We get a daily paper, <u>Stars & Stripes</u>, which is published over here for us. It carries all the news and sports (!) just like a stateside paper. There are also some magazines like <u>Time</u>, <u>Sports Illustrated</u>, <u>Look</u>, <u>Life</u>, etc., if you're lucky enough to get your hands on them...

Luv, Pete

*   *   *

26 Aug 69

Dear Donna,

...Remember that U.S.O. show I was telling you about in my last letter? Well, wouldn't you know it, half way through the show, rockets started raining into Camp Eagle. The sirens started wailing, and everyone beat a hasty exit to the

bunkers. *It so happened the girls of the show wound up in the same bunker as a lot of us officers, so that helped to make things interesting. After the first barrage, a few of us, like dumb nuts, crawled on top of the bunker to watch the "fireworks." The whole sky outside the perimeter was lit up like day with flares. The gunships were hitting the suspected enemy positions with rockets and mini-gun fire. It was all quite interesting, although a little weird. I don't know how much damage was done, but I do know there were some casualties on the other side of Camp Eagle. Our Varsity company area didn't take any hits...*

Love, Pete

Chapter 9

*A man can do nothing better than
to...find satisfaction in his work.
This too, I see, is from the hand of
God...*

--Ecclesiastes 2:24 (NIV)

29 August 1969

"Sir, it's time to wake up."

I stirred, then grunted, and listened as best I could about who would be flying with me, what our tail number was, etc.

0530, that's just way too early, I thought to myself. But of course I rolled out of bed, washed up, shaved, got dressed, and ate some breakfast.

I was at the aircraft before 0630 and pulled our preflight inspection along with my AC. By 0700 we were airborne, with the AC flying the first load: a sling load of two water bladders (rubberized containers which each held around five hundred gallons) to a mountain firebase. As we got close to our destination, I made contact with the firebase: "Pathfinder Rakkasson, Varsity 101."

"Roger Varsity, this is Pathfinder Rakkasson."

"We're hauling some water for you."

"Got you in sight. You are clear to come in with your load."

"Okay, go ahead and pop your smoke."

"Popping smoke."

In a moment I saw purple smoke curling up from a point on the firebase: "Roger, got your goofy grape."

"Goofy grape it is."

After the load had been set down and released, we departed and headed back to the staging area for our next load. "Okay, go ahead and take the next load," said the AC on the intercom.

I put my hands on the flight controls and said, "I got the aircraft."

"You got it," replied the AC and then released his hold on the controls. This little ritual provided clear communication between pilots and ensured someone always had positive control of the aircraft.

"Sir, okay if I tune in AFVN on the FM radio?" the flight engineer asked the AC.

"Sure."

After the flight engineer tuned in AFVN, I flipped on my FM receiver switch so I could listen as well and immediately heard familiar rock music which was oddly pleasant and comforting.

As I brought the aircraft down on approach to the supply staging area, I spotted a loader standing on a stack of artillery ammo boxes which were enfolded in a net. As he awaited our approach, the loader had a fabric "donut" in his hand—attached to a cargo strap which in turn was attached to the cargo net—ready to attach it to our cargo hook. When we were almost at a hover, the flight engineer, who at this time was lying on his stomach on the cargo floor and looking out the cargo hole in the bottom of the Chinook, said: "Got your load in sight. Down three, right two, forward twenty."

Since I couldn't see the load underneath me and to my front, the flight engineer had to be my eyes. I formed a mental image of the instructions he had given me and moved the aircraft in consonance with them.

"Down one, forward ten, forward five ...okay, you're over the load. Hold; hold. ...Load is attached. ...Man is clear of the load. Bring 'er up. ...Strap is tight."

As soon as the slack went out of the cargo strap, the aircraft had the familiar feel of being anchored to the ground. From this point until we got the eight-thousand-pound load airborne, it would require much more power from the two engines. As I pulled up on the thrust lever, the AC manned the beep switch to add power and keep the rotor RPM constant.

"Load is getting light. Load is off the ground," continued the flight engineer.

The next flight maneuver, transitioning to forward movement from a hover, required even more power. I gently moved the cyclic stick forward, and the nose dipped slightly as the aircraft began to move forward. At the same time, I pulled up a little more on the thrust lever to increase power and keep the aircraft from losing altitude. As my airspeed passed twenty knots, I felt the familiar slight vibration and altitude increase as the aircraft encountered translational lift. As we headed back to Firebase Rakkasson we continued our climb to the flight altitude of fifteen hundred feet AGL (above ground level) and airspeed of eighty knots which was normal for a sling load. Without an external load we generally cruised at 120 knots or above.

We were over the coastal plain but would soon be above the mountains which loomed a few miles to our front. As the sun rose higher in the sky behind us, it provided a dazzling display of brilliance on the landscape below. The bright greens of the plain yielded to the distinctly darker green and tawny tones of the peaks and ridges which abruptly thrust upward from the lowlands. My body and mind experienced the pleasant sensations of being on currents of air above this incredible vista of enchanting beauty and vastness spread out below me—earth and sky reaching out toward each other until they met at the far-off hazy horizon.

My reverie was broken by radio transmissions as we neared our destination. "Pathfinder Rakkasson, Varsity 101," my AC (we called him Bear) growled over the UHF radio.

"Go ahead, 101."

"Got some ammo for you."

"Rog, the winds are picking up. They are 240 at fifteen knots, gusting to twenty-five."

We'd been feeling the turbulence since we got over the high country. I wanted to do a good approach. I felt like I was getting the hang of mountain flying, but then I'd only been at it a couple weeks so I sorely lacked experience. Rakkasson was on a narrow ridgeline that ran roughly northwest to southeast. The mountain dropped away steeply to the southwest and the northeast. I set up my approach to the southwest a little higher than normal. If I came in too shallow, we risked getting caught in the downdrafts that occurred on the lee side of the ridge. However, coming in steeper meant that the rate of descent would also be higher and would require more power to terminate the descent at a hover over the firebase. On top of that, our density altitude was high again that day, and the higher the density altitude, the less lift we had. One good thing—we'd been burning off our load of fuel which lightened our gross weight.

I could see the firebase in front of me, a brown scar on the ridgeline. Someone on the firebase popped a smoke grenade, and I saw the yellow smoke marking the area for the load drop. I kept my approach speed low to lessen the power required to stop our descent and bring us to a hover over the firebase. The turbulence was really bouncing us around. As we got close to the ground, I gradually slowed my airspeed and rate of descent by pulling back on the cyclic and up the thrust lever. Bear was working the beep switch to increase power and thus maintain our all-important rotor RPM. I could see a G.I. ahead of me, giving me hand signals of where to deposit my load.

The flight engineer again became my eyes: "Got your drop zone in sight. Forward fifty, down twenty, right five."

I breathed a sigh of relief as I came to a hover over the drop zone. We'd had the power to safely terminate our approach at a hover.

"You're over the drop point. Bring 'er down. ...Five, three, two, one. ...Load is on the ground. Give me some slack. ...Load is released."

"Clear on the left," said the left door gunner.

"Clear on the right," chimed in the other gunner.

With eight thousand pounds less weight, and the updrafts on the windward side of the ridge as we took off, the Chinook literally jumped into the air as if all power restraints were cast off.

"Not bad," said the AC. That was the best affirmation I could have hoped for. I got a big grin on my face.

After a few minutes Bear said, "I got the aircraft."

"You got it," I verified.

The tension drained out of me and my muscles relaxed. I lit a cigarette and took a big drag. As I did, I once again wondered why I ever started that nasty habit. I had gone all the way through high school and my one-plus year of college without ever lighting up, even while some of my friends had become accomplished smokers. I guess it had happened at boot camp where I'd often heard the familiar words of the drill sergeant at the start of a short break: "Smoke 'em if you got 'em!" I didn't have any on me, but I usually bummed one.

Finally one of the guys had said, "Hey Petersen, when are you going to buy your own cigarettes?" So I had.

We picked up another load and headed for Firebase Currahee in the Ashau Valley. The valley was about thirty-five miles long, north to south, and just a couple miles from the Laos border in places. Because of its remote location and rugged terrain, as well as elephant grass up to fifteen feet tall on the valley floor, the Ashau had been a major infiltration route for the bad guys and their supplies from Laos and North Vietnam into the northern part of South Vietnam. Earlier in the spring and summer of 1969, the 101st had fought some major battles in and around the Ashau, including the battle for Hamburger Hill. The Ashau continued to be a major focus of the division into the Fall of 1969, which meant most of our missions were in support of firebases and troops in the same area.

On our final approach into Currahee, the pathfinder all of a sudden starting yelling: "Circle to the echo, circle to the echo! Code word pig is in effect!"

Bear had turned off his radio receiver, so I relayed the message to him over the intercom. He just said, "Huh?" and continued his final approach and dropped off the load. After taking off again, he contacted the pathfinder to find out what was going on while I took over control of the aircraft. Apparently they'd taken some rockets and mortars in the previous few minutes. Bear just chuckled and said: "Never heard of code word pig before."

I headed for a forward supply point not far from the valley.

Bear cautioned, "There's a lot of sand and dirt at our load pick-up point. Don't come in too slow, and bring it to a low hover so we don't have a total brown-out."

I did as he told me. As I came close to the ground, the rotor wash caused a ferocious dust storm, but I was able to keep that all-important visual contact with the ground. The wind velocity coming off the rotor blades was estimated to be well over one hundred mph, so no one was very excited about getting close to a hovering Chinook in a dusty LZ (landing zone). After my load was hooked up, I didn't waste much time getting it off the ground and gaining some altitude to get us above the blowing dust. I wanted to make sure I was never responsible for crashing a Chinook by losing all visual reference to the ground.

Later we shut down in a LZ so the chief could do an aircraft inspection. We took advantage of the time for a quick lunch of cold C-rations. Being a new guy, I learned an important lesson that day—never eat the pork meal cold. When I opened the can, I was greeted by congealed fat floating in some nasty looking broth which covered the supposedly cooked pork. I was hungry enough that I averted my view of the can's contents as best I could and downed it as quickly as possible. After that I immediately opened my cheese tin which I spread on crackers. The cheese and crackers as well as the tin of bread pudding (at least I think that's what it was) helped to cover up the unpleasant experience of the cold pork. Just as I finished, I observed the flight engineer doing C-rations the right way: he started the Chinook's APU, then held a can of Cs with a long-handled wrench up to the exhaust port of the APU to take advantage of its high exhaust gas temperatures. In just a few seconds he had a hot meal of C-rations.

We were soon in the air again, "humping" more loads throughout the afternoon. As the day wore on, my hind quarters got sorer. We had high winds and severe turbulence which bounced the helicopter around at times like an untamed ping-pong ball, and made the flying very tiring.

Finally, the last load of the day had been delivered, and we headed back to Camp Eagle. "Eagle Tower, Varsity 101."

"Varsity 101, Eagle Tower."

"Varsity 101 is at Square City [the Citadel of Hue] for the refueling pads."

"Roger Varsity 101. Winds are two five zero at ten knots with gusts to eighteen. Altimeter setting is two niner niner five. You are clear for approach to the refueling point."

"Roger, thank you."

All the refueling pads were being used, but after hovering for a couple minutes, a slick vacated a pad and we were able to set down and get topped off. After getting tower clearance, we flew the one-minute hop over to the Locker Room, hovered into an empty revetment, set down, and went through the shutdown procedure. I peeled myself from my seat, waited while Bear filled out the paperwork, and walked the short distance to my hootch.

I relaxed with an ice cold beer from the mini-refrigerator Phil and I had been able to purchase from the PX. We'd also been able to get some beer in aluminum cans. Prior to this, all we had been able to get was old Carling Black Label that existed from before the time of aluminum beer cans and had been sitting around long enough for rust to form on the cans. I read the newspaper before going to see a movie at our outdoor theater. After that it was shower time and to bed. Another long day was over.

Chapter 10

*A cheerful look brings joy to the
heart,
and good news gives health to the
bones.*

--Proverbs 15:30 (NIV)

2 Sept. 69

Dear Donna,

I was shocked, flabbergasted, and <u>very</u> happily surprised yesterday. Why? Well, guess how many pieces of mail I got from you? Not one, not two, not even three. Would you believe <u>FIVE</u>? I just could not believe it, I was so overjoyed with them...You'd best believe I was envied by the other guys around here...

I love hearing from you in your letters...I find them very satisfying, informative, and thoroughly enjoyable[.] I love hearing your ideas, thoughts, and feelings. You have such a fresh, youthful, and frank approach to everything...

*　　　*　　　*

8 Sept. 69

Dear Donna,

...It was so good to hear from you again today. I can't stress enough how much a difference in morale it makes to receive mail from home and people close to me. I was always glad to get mail in the States, but it was nothing like it means to me over here. It's almost like mail is a necessary ingredient to leading a sane, nearly normal life. So far, the many miles of separation from my "other" life and the prospect of being separated from this for a year hasn't really gotten me down. I think a big factor has been my mail. I really don't deserve all the attention I've been getting from you, but am <u>very</u> happy with it...

Hey, that was real good to "meet" your family in your letter yesterday. I'll introduce you to mine. Sharon is the oldest and needs no introduction [because Sharon's and

75

Donna's families belonged to the same church]. Don (24) is my big brother who always used to beat me up when we were little kids. He's not big enough anymore. I think you've seen him before. He just got out of the Navy and will be going back to college.

After me comes Nancy (19). She went to Calvin [College] last year and will be going to my alma mater, U. of Wash. in Seattle, this year with a major in nursing. I think maybe you've seen her before.

Next is Shirley (16). She is my dear little mentally retarded sister. She went to Children's Retreat [institution for the mentally retarded] in G.R. [Grand Rapids, MI] when she was younger. Now she goes to a special school near Tacoma, Wash. She's a smart little whip for someone like her.

Last, but not at all the least, [come] the three younger boys, Karl (13), Kenny (12), and Keith (9). It's hard to believe that those kids are that old. I watched them all grow up and have always been "big brother" to them. They'll always be my baby brothers. I feel like I had a hand in raising them; I used to spend hours playing with them. I guess that's why I love little kids so much. I even taught them all to walk!

There, you've met my family. I think I was very fortunate in having been raised in a large family. It did mean some sacrifices through the years, but we had a special kind of happiness and togetherness. You should've seen us when we all got together at Christmas. That was one of the happiest times of my life. I think I'll get hit worst with homesickness and loneliness at Christmas time this year. Oh well, I'm supposed to be an adult now who doesn't let things like that get him down. It doesn't always work that way, though. Enough of that!

It's getting late so I'd better get some sleep. Ho Chi Minh [North Vietnamese leader] is dead so we're in the middle of [a] three-day truce. Maybe with his death the war [will] be scaled down, although I really doubt it. The weather is starting to move into the Ashau and parts of the mountains. We couldn't get into some of the firebases [for] a couple of days because they were socked in, enshrouded with clouds. The last couple days I've been flying to Da Nang on the bus run. It's just what it means — we bus people back and forth, just like our Chinooks were Greyhounds. Oh well, it's fun, easy-type flying...

Love, Pete

P.S. I was able to go to chapel yesterday. It was an extra special uplift because we had communion services. It meant a lot to me.

*   *   *

14 Sept. 69

Dear Donna,

...It's already one of those pleasant days. The temp. is near a warming 100°, and the humidity is around a comfortable 90%. Of course, there is no breeze at all to disturb these comforts. The air is nicely close and stifling; I have to gasp to get any oxygen. The bodd manages to stay wet and miserable. In other words: LET ME OUT OF HERE!

No, it's not always as bad as I described it. We usually have nice breezes to ventilate the place. Like last night: my poor bare skin was getting so "cold" that I had to pull a sheet over my bodd! It does rain every once in awhile, and that does cool things down. When I'm flying I can always keep cool, because we can get plenty of ventilation in the cockpit. Besides, it's cooler in the mountains and at the higher altitudes we fly.

...I had a great day yesterday...I got to watch a <u>football</u> game! I'm about the biggest football and sports nut that the U.S. has ever produced. One of my buddies has a TV, and the Armed Forces Network showed the Chicago Bears-Green Bay Packers exhibition game which was played a couple weeks ago. I can't begin to tell you how good it was to see a football game again. That was one of the hardest things for me about coming to Vietnam — I have to miss football season...

We also had the highlight of the day — a live USO show. It was a Filipino group, but they were pretty good. Among some of the songs they played were "We Gotta Get Out of this Place" and "I Wanna Go Home." That's kinda hard to take. They were good, but of course, no show could be as good as a football game...

*   *   *

18 Sept. 69

Dear Donna,

[Responding to a recent letter from Donna]...I just can't believe what goes on in high schools nowadays. I always thought most of the freaks were college kids or dropout types. I guess I've been away from high school too long. That kinda makes me ancient, right? After all, I just turned 21, so that makes me just a cog in the nameless throng of the IBM card Establishment. No, I don't really feel that way. Part of the reason I joined the Army was so that I could do something different, see more of the diversified aspects of life and land. It has given me more of an awareness of people and things, a very good learning experience. After all, how much of the "outside world" [does one] see living in a sheltered Dutch community? I think the best thing it's done for me, though, is helped me to a greater awareness of my God. I tended to take church and religion too much for granted when I was surrounded by it. It was also a good maturing process and taught me to shift for myself. I did learn to do things for myself quite young, though, being from a large family. Do you know that I had my own newspaper route when I was seven years old? I can hardly believe that now, looking back. I was such a little kid: the bag which I carried my newspapers in, slung over my shoulder, used to almost drag the ground. Yep, I used to carry those good old papers in South Dakota (where we lived until I was 16) through the 110° summer and the -20° cold of winter. I have many good memories of it.

     That little description you had in your letter that I got a couple days ago — about the beautiful fall weather, washing the car, going to football games, etc. — put a touch of melancholy in me. I started dreaming that I was back home in my favorite season — nights were frosty, the days were cool, crisp, and clear. Leaves were changing to their brilliant reds, golds, and browns, and floating lazily to the ground. After I had raked up the leaves, I spent long afternoons stomping through the cornfields and pastures with my shotgun, pheasant hunting. Then I would bundle up and go to the Friday night football game. The air was exhilarating and bracing; everything I did gave me the feeling of freedom, like a carefree bird. Then I awoke out of my dream and came back to reality. Suddenly, I was uncomfortable — sweat was beading on my face and back. The air was too damp to evaporate the wetness of my body. I *couldn't get rid of the oppressive heat. What happened to the crisp fall air? Oh, yes, I got transported back to the tropics…*

*   *   *

21 Sept. 69

Dear Donna,

    I'll start this letter now, but I probably will have to finish it later this afternoon or evening. We flew a couple hours this morning, but had to come down [just] now because of a faulty transmission oil temp. gauge. It'll probably be a half hour before it's fixed.

    Yesterday was the first full day of flying this week. We had about three dark days with heavy rains. Friday, I had to fly a couple hours in that "soup." It was a tactical emergency[:] a firebase in the mountains was critically short of ammo. So here we were, flying through ravines and valleys, dodging mountain ridges and trying to stay out of the clouds. The visibility was terrible because of the rain and mist — we had everything we could do to see where we were going and keep from running into the side of a mountain. Well, we made it alright, but it does help to increase the pucker factor.

    Yesterday (Sat.), the weather cleared somewhat, so we flew most of the day. We pulled out a couple fire bases in the northern end of the Ashau Valley in some of the most rugged and beautiful terrain I've ever seen. You see, the only way these fire bases have of getting supplies is by helicopter. Well, the monsoon season is approaching, and that means the mountains will be socked in with clouds and bad weather for months, almost all winter long. So, in a couple weeks <u>all</u> friendly forces will have been pulled back toward the coastal plains, giving almost all the mountain areas back to the gooks.

Then, come next March or April, we will once again have to put our troops back in there, and once again they will have to secure it from the enemy. In the process, more husbands, fathers, and sons will be killed in this never-ending, vicious cycle. I told myself before I left home that I was going to try to keep from airing my negative attitudes to my friends and loved-ones back home. But sometimes the utter stupidity of this war gets to me. All it is, is two opposing forces trying to get a bigger body count than the other force. How many homes have been saddened by the loss of loved ones is something I would not care to think about. If we had pulled out of here a couple years ago, it would have been a disaster. The way the situation is now is also a disaster. It's a hopeless dilemma.

The results of this war were driven home to me yesterday. It all seems so more real now. I was reading through the Army Times last night and happened across the weekly obituary column. There, under the heading of "Missing and Presumed Dead" was the name of one of my best buddies in flight school. I had lost contact with him a few weeks ago and couldn't figure out why. Now I know. It hit me terribly hard; I didn't sleep much last night...

In spite of this situation here, I'm still enjoying my "job" because I'm flying. It's still so very interesting because everything is so varied. Like yesterday, something new again. Here we were, soaring through these ominous cloud layers, waiting for an opening in the clouds through which to descend. It was almost like we were playing a game of tag or football with the clouds. It was all so starkly beautiful. Then, on clear days, I just climb and climb into the vast blue, nothing holding me down, as God's beautiful creation unfolds beneath me. It's such a feeling of exhilaration, of complete freedom...

*   *   *

29 Sept. 69

Dear Donna,

    The last couple days we've had the most miserable weather since I've been in country. We've had temperatures of over 105°, and the humidity has me crawling the walls. The nights are pleasantly cool, though. We've even had beautiful moons the last few days. Such enchanting, romantic, evenings! Heck of a lot of good that does me. Spending it with the same old ugly guys — really a swinging time. I'd better suppress my complaints, though — I've still got almost ten more months of the same old thing...

Chapter 11

...the heavens poured down rain...

--Psalm 68:8 (NIV)

3 October 1969

It had rained all night long. I was beginning to wonder if the wet monsoons had arrived early this year. It felt good to be cool enough to have a blanket over me in my bunk. In fact, it was almost chilly. Maybe I'd be able to stay in bed longer this morning. Maybe we wouldn't be flying today, but then I couldn't count on that.

The past couple days had been dark and rainy, but we'd been flying in that crap. Two days ago we pulled out the last loads of the last firebase in the mountains around the Ashau Valley. It had been a scary experience for me because I hadn't had much time flying in that kind of weather. We had to fly low-level and very slow, along an old dirt road, so we wouldn't get lost or inadvertently go into the "soup" and jeopardize our safety. It had been raining hard, and the low clouds and fog caused very poor visibility. We came too close to trees and a hillside on a couple of occasions. And flying that low and slow made us sitting ducks for any bad guys who might be around. But then Charlie had a problem, too, since he'd most likely be down in thick jungle, so he'd catch only a momentary glimpse of us when we flew low-level.

When we had gotten that last load out of there we had breathed a sigh of relief, thinking we could go home. No such thing. One of the Cobra gunships that was flying cover and escort for us had been shot down earlier in the day. The crew had been rescued, but we had to go

out there again and lift the gunship back to "civilization."
I had flown with a UH-1 "Huey" slung below me before,
but this was a first with an AH-1G "Cobra." Hueys
streamlined nicely as a sling load, with minimal
oscillation. Not so the Cobra. I had heard war stories
about how Cobras would crab, or ride sideways, at a 30°
angle or worse, so one couldn't fly over thirty knots
because the oscillation would get too bad. Fortunately
there was a drogue chute attached to the tail of the Cobra
which streamlined and stabilized it on the flight home.

I heard the door of the hootch next to us open and
footsteps falling across the floor.

"Sir?" came the voice of the ops clerk.

"YEAH, WHAT DO YOU WANT?" Bear's voice
reverberated angrily.

I felt kinda sorry for the clerk, but then I was
hoping he wouldn't open Phil's and my door either. Bear
was actually a very nice guy, he just didn't like being
awakened. After that I could hear muffled voices but
couldn't hear what was being said. Without a doubt,
Bear was getting his missions for the day.

After a short period of silence, I heard our door
open and saw the familiar beam of light from a flashlight.
The footsteps stopped by my bunk.

"Mr. Petersen?" My heart sank a little. I was
flying again today.

After getting my mission info, the clerk walked
over to Phil's bunk and said, "Mr. Lanza?" Phil was
flying today as well.

I did my usual routine of washing up and shaving, then put on my poncho and walked over to the mess hall for a breakfast of scrambled powdered eggs and toast. By the time I got back to my hootch, the rain had almost stopped except for some light drizzle. I went out to the aircraft, did the preflight inspection along with my AC, and we were soon in the air headed north.

The Marines were being pulled out of northern I Corps. Their AO had been mainly in Quang Tri Province which bumped up against the DMZ. The 101st Division's primary AO had been in Thua Thien Province, just south of Quang Tri Province, but with the Marine pullout, we were expanding to cover up to the DMZ. The First ARVN Division (Army of the Republic of Vietnam) also was being given major responsibilities there, and we would be supporting them as well. Except for the coastal plain, Quang Tri Province was just as mountainous as the area around the Ashau. Probably the most well-known spot in Quang Tri Province was Khe Sanh, the site of major battles and a 2½-month siege during the 1968 Tet Offensive. [Tet, the Vietnamese Lunar New Year beginning 30 January 1968, saw the outbreak of coordinated North Vietnamese Army/Viet Cong (NVA/VC) attacks throughout much of South Vietnam.] In late 1969, there was nothing to it except a lot of dirt, the remains of an airstrip, and a lot of battle-scarred terrain.

After a +20-minute flight from Camp Eagle, we arrived at a forward supply point near Quang Tri City and started hauling loads into various firebases. In one early sortie, we hauled troops instead of a sling load. We could pack thirty-three U.S. troops into a Chinook—there were thirty-three troop seats in a Chinook, and American commanders wanted each troop fastened into a seat. Normally the seats were folded up against either side of the cargo bay when we were hauling cargo, which was most of the time. But they could be folded down pretty quickly if we had a load of troops. I learned that if we were carrying Vietnamese troops, their commanders usually wanted us to pack as many into a Chinook as possible. They wanted the seats in their stowed position, then they'd jam their guys in on the floor. The Vietnamese tended to be smaller than G.I.s and they carried less gear, so we could transport about seventy ARVNs at one time.

For the rest of that day, we hauled 105-mm artillery pieces into firebases as well as countless sorties of supplies. The weather would deteriorate, then improve. At times we had to wait for breaks in the clouds to get into some of the firebases. The sky seemed to be filled with aircraft. Along with just about every helicopter the Army flew, there were also Marine CH-46s—which looked like baby Chinooks (both were made by Boeing Vertol)—and CH-53 "Jolly Green Giants."

As we were approaching a firebase, the left door gunner said, "Sir, there's a fast mover at our eight o'clock, passing us on our left."

I turned my head to the left in time to see an Air Force F-4 Phantom fighter hurrying ahead of us. As he got a few hundred yards to our front, he released two napalm canisters from his wing weapons stores which tumbled through the air toward the thick jungle canopy below. In a few seconds the canisters hit the ground and burst into an orange conflagration. The billowing of the smoke was an indicator of the fierceness of the fire. An involuntary shudder coursed through my body; I quickly tried to focus on our current mission.

A little while later, we heard a familiar message on Guard: "This is Hotel on Guard. Arty mission commencing 1530 hours for one five minutes, max ord [maximum elevation of the ordnance] nine thousand feet." In addition, map coordinates were provided.

"That's going off in five minutes. Better check it out," said the AC.

I quickly pulled out the map and checked the coordinates. "That's just about where we are now, a little to our west. We should be clear of it in a minute."

"Like we didn't have enough air traffic already."

Intelligence reports we'd gotten a few days ago said this AO near the DMZ was crawling with Charlie. But then what area in Nam wasn't? What I didn't understand was why we were putting more grunts and cannon cockers out in the mountains now. We'd just gotten through pulling troops out of the Ashau area because the monsoons were on their way and we wouldn't be able to support them from the air. If we couldn't support those troops because of the bad weather conditions, how were we going to be able to support these guys? I let the question fall to the back of my mind, once again required to do my duty without fully understanding all the whys.

It was raining when we landed back at Camp Eagle late in the afternoon. After getting some hot chow, I did what I usually did that time of the day—I went to see the evening movie. Raindrops splattered on my poncho while I tried to keep the rain out of my eyes so I could see the movie. Drip, drip, drip off the brim of my hat and onto my rain pants. I stayed mostly dry, except that the weather was so damp that my body was feeling clammy long before the movie was over. I was ready for Romeo and Juliet to do themselves in so I could get back to my hootch.

The next day there was a steady rain. We didn't launch any birds, but a few were on stand-by. I wasn't on any of them because I had duty as officer of the guard that night. Each sector of the Camp Eagle perimeter was the responsibility of a unit or group of units, and Varsity was no exception. A number of bunkers were manned by our enlisted men that evening, and I was in a command post. As I reported for duty, my main thought was of the Saturday night cookout the rest of the guys were enjoying and the succulent steaks I was missing. I wasn't feeling too tired, which was good since I had to stay up all night. After I had done my initial comm checks with my bunkers and called in my first situation report (sitrep) to higher headquarters' CP (Command Post) I had my driver take me in a jeep to visit each of the bunkers. All the guys seemed alert and had all the gear they were supposed to have. GIs at each bunker challenged me like they were supposed to, and I didn't forget the password they were listening for. I did think it was rather comical, though, since I was pretty sure Charlie had yet to drive up to one of our bunkers in a jeep.

After a couple hours, I again got in the jeep, but this time I was going to just one bunker. Every night on the perimeter, a commander would randomly select a few bunkers at different times of the night to blow off one of their claymore mines. A claymore was a curve-shaped device with hundreds of steel balls on the convex side and a charge of C-4 explosive behind the balls. This night one of our bunkers had been selected.

"Okay, guys, you get to blow a claymore."

"Cool! Do we do it now?"

"Yeah, let's make sure everyone is away from the slit opening. ...Okay, let's do it."

The specialist in charge of the bunker picked up one of the detonators, kneeled down, and activated it. The explosion ripped through the air. Even as I was sitting on the floor of the bunker, the concussion reached every part of my body with the strangest sense of impact, like some of the air had been sucked out of the bunker and a powerful force had hit me. In a moment it was past.

"Cool!"

"I wish there had been a gook in the wire right then."

"Can you believe what that claymore would've done to him?"

"Okay, men, you still have guard duty for the rest of night. Stay alert," I cautioned. My driver and I headed back to the CP.

"Sir, you want me to drop you off and get some coffee for the guys from the mess hall?"

"Yeah, good idea. Come back and pick me up and I'll go out with you to bring it to the guys."

After the coffee had been distributed and I had called in a couple more hourly sitreps, the silence of the CP was interrupted by a ringing phone. "Sir, I think I see something out front of the bunker, beyond the wire."

"What is it?"

"Well, I can't tell, maybe a guy."

"Are you using your night vision scope?"

"Yeah."

"Is he moving?"

"That's the thing, I don't think so. Just seems to be sitting there."

"How long you been watching him?"

"Oh, quite awhile, don't know how long."

"Okay, I'll come have a look."

Oh, man, that's the last thing I want, I thought to myself. *Let's just keep it quiet and get through the night.* "Okay, we need to take a little trip out to a bunker," I said to my driver. The rain had not let up since I

91

reported for duty earlier that evening. In fact, it seemed to be coming down harder. What a miserable night.

After we arrived at the bunker, I asked, "Is he still out there?"

"Yeah, I think so."

"Okay, let me have a look. Where is he?" I pointed the scope in the direction he indicated. The greenish glow of the night scope made it hard to see anything at first. I guessed that the rain wasn't helping things at all. As my eyes got accustomed to it, I could see the rolls of concertina wire and other barbed wire that were stretched out in front of the main fence in front of the bunker. I slowly swept the whole area in front of me, looking for anything out of the ordinary. I could see trees at some distance beyond the perimeter, and a number of bushes or other vegetation between the trees and the wire. I couldn't see anything to get excited about. "Okay, take the scope and find what you were looking at and then let me look at it to make sure we're looking at the same thing."

"Okay. ...I see it, it still hasn't moved. Maybe I'm just seeing things."

"Don't worry about that." I took the scope back in order to try again to see what he saw. "Okay, I think I've got it now. I'll just watch it for awhile."

I couldn't really make out what it was – maybe a stump, or possibly a bush, but it didn't seem like a person. Yet I didn't want to be too quick to write it off, because I didn't really know either. I watched it for a long time, but there simply was no movement. "You know, I just don't think we have someone there. But keep an eye on it, and don't hesitate to blow a claymore or use your weapons if it moves."

As we drove back to the CP, I said to the driver, "Better make another coffee run."

Morning finally came without any more excitement. After I was relieved of my post, I headed out in the rain to get some breakfast at the mess hall, after which I was going to sleep as long as I could. It seemed that instead of the rain letting up, the heavens had just opened up and let loose—that the previous days of rain were merely a prelude to the downpour we were experiencing now. But I wasn't too worried about the weather just then. All I wanted to was sleep.

There seemed to be a lot of commotion in my dream, and I could sense a lot of noise and confusion. After a few moments I realized it wasn't a dream... I was awakening. It was still daylight: my watch told me it was mid-afternoon. The rain was still pounding on the roof like it had been when I'd gone to sleep that morning. I got up to see what was going on. Pulling on my raingear, I went outside. As I turned the corner of the officer hootches, headed for the outhouse, I got quite a surprise. Our little valley, winding its way through our company's area, was gone. The tiny creek had become a raging flood of boiling, churning waters.

Just then, one of the guys appeared: "The enlisted men's barracks are flooded! We need all the help we can get to move them to higher ground!"

I made it over to them as quickly as I could. I couldn't see a single barracks that wasn't under at least some water. I could see a lot of bedding and personal items which had been hastily moved away from the water's edge.

"Watch for snakes and rats!" someone was saying. "We've seen some already!"

I joined the mad rush to get stuff to higher ground. "No more wading into the stream! We've already had a couple guys swept downstream!" someone was yelling.

"Anyone missing?" yelled another.

"Not to my knowledge! We got those guys out!"

There was a lot of water in the barracks, but at least there wasn't a current. I was already wet above my knees. For the next couple hours we just kept hauling stuff out of those barracks to the highest ground within reach. Some of the barracks had been anchored down to keep them from floating away. Every single one of the twenty-two barracks was under as much as three or four feet of water. The chaos of nonstop pouring rain, rushing waters, and gear strewn everywhere, combined with our attempts to get those men and their belongings to higher ground, made for a rather frightening experience.

While some of the guys salvaged their possessions, many lost TVs, radios, stereos, tape decks, etc. The flood meant that there were over two hundred homeless men.

Cots were set up in our big hangar for temporary quarters. The officers were fortunate in that the flood waters got within three feet of their hootches before it stopped rising. It kept raining for several more days, but the creek didn't rise anymore. Rainfall figures several days later would show that we got over twenty inches of rain that Sunday (5 October). The Camp Eagle rainfall totals for the first eight days of October were 57.9 inches of rain. Even in Washington where my home was, I don't think we ever got over fifty inches of rain in a year!

We weren't the only ones hit by the deluge. The entire coastal plains of northern I Corps experienced flooding that October. Most of the roads were flooded, bringing traffic to a standstill. We pilots got in very little flying, especially during that first week, when the rain was worst. Near the end of the week we did manage to get up in the air on a couple different days, mainly to help some of the local populace. The first day we evacuated a couple of villages with our Chinooks. This included transporting everything you could think of — papa-sans, mama-sans, baby-sans, pigs, chickens, personal items, etc. I'd never seen anything like it before. I felt like I was flying Noah's Ark.

The next day we carried tons and tons of rice into beleaguered villages up and down the coastal plain corridor. One never knew which ones of these villages were VC sympathizers, and some of them may have even harbored VC, either voluntarily or not. But at least it seemed from the expressions on their faces that they were genuinely pleased and grateful to get some help in the way of food supplies.

It felt good to be in the air again, especially for the purpose of doing some "good deeds."

* * *

8 Oct. 69

Dear Donna,

...Camp Eagle hadn't [gotten] hit with rockets or mortars in almost two months. Well, two nights ago, right when we're having all the trouble with floods and rain, here come the mortars.

Charlie put quite a few in the sector next to ours, although none in ours. We spent over two hours in that damp, wet bunker on the red alert. This kind of weather is what the gooks like to fight in. Camp Eagle has been taking sniper fire for the past couple nights. Nothing's been hit — it's just more or less harassment. Up north along the DMZ our grunts are in some heavy contact at times. I guess ol' Chuck still wants to fight. I haven't flown up by the DMZ in over a week now.

Must go now. I have much to do. I'm trying to figure out a way to dry my clothes so I won't catch pneumonia. Oh well, if I get sick enough, they'll probably send me home...

Love, Dale

Chapter 12

*Their feet run to evil,
and they make haste to shed innocent
blood...*

--Isaiah 59:7 (KJV)

Oct. 14

Dear Donna,

Today is my first day up in four days. You see, that weather really got to me in the form of one of the worst head colds I've ever had. Well, I swallowed my pride and went to the flight surgeon. He gave me lots of good pills and put me on bed rest for three days. It's extra dangerous flying with a head cold, mainly because you have so much trouble with equalizing the pressure in your ears and run the risk of permanently damaging them. I don't want any of that!

...One thing about this weather – it's nicely cool, even if it is so damp. This morning the sun is out and they're predicting 95° temperatures. No happy medium here, just one extreme to the next.

...The enlisted men are moving back into their barracks. I've never seen such a mess of mud and filth... The roads around here are one big bed of muck. I've never seen such a sloppy mess in my life, I saw many vehicles stuck up to their axles in the stuff.

...Well, after a week without any mail, it all hit at once. If I've counted correctly, I've gotten <u>nine</u> cards and letters from you in the past five days. I'm flabbergasted! I don't know what to say...I just want to make sure that you know how much it means to me, and how much easier it makes things over here for me.

I'll try to answer some of your questions...

I was rather shocked about your confrontation with the SDS [Students for Democratic Society]. Naïve old me didn't realize that SDS was so prevalent in high schools. I had seen quite a bit of them when I was at college. They are about the most hypocritical group I've ever seen. They protest against war, violence, police brutality, etc. And yet, they have, next to the Black Panthers, caused more riots, and thus have caused many injuries and deaths, than any other group over the past few years. No, [like you, I] don't agree with a lot of the things about this war. But I also think Nixon is doing just about everything he can to end this thing. If everyone would support him in his efforts, I think the war would be ended sooner. The Commies are just holding out because of the dissension. As far as the GIs in Vietnam go, most of them would like the war to end soon. But no one I know over here appreciates the protestors. We don't consider them [to be] helping us with their protests. All they do, in effect, is cause more US casualties. The Commies think that the US will capitulate to the dissenters, so why should they negotiate for peace?

And how do those dimwits think I could have avoided coming here? Oh yes, I could have exiled myself in Canada. I could have refused to be inducted and [could] now be serving out a prison term. I would've had a great future ahead of me. Not only would my future have been blighted, but worse yet, I would've had my conscience to live with rest of my life.

And anyone who has support or sympathy for the Viet Cong is truly sick. They say that the VC are fighting for the people of Vietnam, to liberate them and give them a better life...[S]ome of the mass graves [were] being uncovered near Hue a few weeks ago. I'm sure that those more than 3,000 people who were methodically massacred [during the 1968 Tet Offensive] were real grateful to the VC for what they did for them...

Yes, there are many dilemmas to this war. But I think people should be real careful who they are pointing accusing fingers at.

I'm sorry for telling you all this, especially about the Hue victims... It does no good; it only makes life more disgusting and distressing.

...Don't worry about me 'cause I'm plenty fine. In spite of many things, my morale is plenty high and I still can find a lot of enjoyment in life. God bless you.

Love, Dale

*   *   *

17 Oct 69

Dear Donna,

Good evening to you in the land of the big PX, from me in the fun capital of the world. Nope, I'm not in Sydney, Australia or some other exotic place like that. I'm still right here in Camp Eagle, Thua Thien Province, Republic of Vietnam. I'll try to get this written this evening before I go to work. We've got a night mission tonight — don't know what it is yet, but I imagine I'll find out some time. That's about how well informed they keep us around here... They hardly ever call night missions unless there's an urgent necessity for it.

I intensely dislike night flying around here. You see, it's a matter of my wanting to see where I'm going. I really enjoy night flying in the States. There, you take off and land [on] well-lit airfields. Also, [there are] plenty of lights — from towns, radio towers, etc. — which [make] it very easy to navigate. There is something very calm, peaceful, and enjoyable about night flying then. But around here it's an entirely different story. Once you get in the air, it's complete blackness [unless it's a clear night with stars and a good moon]. [There are] absolutely no lights around [on the ground] with which to get your bearings. It makes you feel awfully lost. You can almost feel the blackness.... [Once you get to your destination], you still have to make your landing. Most of the time they'll shine a flashlight [or a strobe light], which you can hardly see. So here you are, making an approach to a little pinpoint light in utter blackness. You more or less just have to "feel" your way down. What's really bad is your depth perception is all screwed up at night and there are no ground references you can see. I've never gotten vertigo (spatial disorientation) yet. You don't dare turn on your landing lights because that makes a beautiful target...

Yesterday I was flying up by the DMZ. We conducted an artillery raid... On an artillery raid, you lift an artillery battery, the crew, and the ammo they need into a specified location in the morning. Our location was two miles from the Laotian border and one mile from the DMZ. That's beautiful, very rugged country, but it sure is a no-man's land. Then, after they shot up all their ammo, we took them out in the late afternoon just as quickly as we put them in. They carry out these kinds of raids when there are intelligence reports of enemy concentrations. Just before we fly in with the artillery pieces, the smaller Hueys carry in a company of infantry who provide security for the artillery team while they are there. Then in we come with gunships flying cover and escort for us. It all works as smoothly as clockwork. We got a "well done" from the division commander (a two-star general) for that mission...

Love, Dale

*   *   *

22 Oct. 69

Dear Donna,

Look at the date. Do you realize that by the time you get this letter, I'll have less than nine months to go? That means that ¼ of my tour is already gone. I'm getting to be an old-timer here already! But I also have ¾ of my tour remaining. Arrghh! Oh well, if I don't start counting days, maybe they'll come a little faster.

...[T]he action has been real light around here, even up by the DMZ. There's a big lull all over Vietnam. I hope it has some significance that maybe everyone is tired of fighting. That's a super-optimistic outlook, though. It could also mean that the gooks are preparing for a big offensive. Only time will tell. There are rumors floating around that Tricky Dick [Nixon] is going to announce a ceasefire in his Nov. 3 speech. I'll have to see it to believe it.

I haven't been doing near as much flying in Vietnam as I thought I would before I came over here. I was under the impression that I'd be flying every day, five to ten hours each day. Well, we don't fly every day. Some days that we do fly, we may fly only a couple hours. Sometimes we do fly eight or ten hours in a day. It varies as much as light and darkness. You can't tell from one day to the next. There are two reasons for this: too many pilots, and just not enough to do around here. I've got a feeling though, that when the monsoon season is over in a few months, they'll be moving new firebases into the mountains all over the place. They'll move into the Ashau Valley again, and we'll have so much flying to do that we won't be able to keep up with it...

Love, Dale

Chapter 13

*…[why is it] that he is trying to take
my life?*

--I Samuel 20:1(NIV)

17 November 1969

Another day of flying. Not that I minded. Time went so much faster when I flew all day, especially if we had several full days of flying in a row. The only problem with flying for many hours at a time was with my hind quarters. In the morning my cockpit seat could feel relatively soft, but by late afternoon it felt like I was sitting on a bunch of rocks.

I was glad to have a new piece of equipment—a new helmet. The Army had recently come out with a new pilot's helmet design. The most noticeable difference was the insulation around the earpieces—the noise from the forward transmission was drastically reduced, so there was no longer any need to wear earplugs. I could hear the radio traffic so much better now. Maybe I wouldn't lose my hearing after all.

The flying I had been doing today hadn't been quite as extensive as it had been on several of the previous days. We had been flying various sorties out of Camp Evans, a supply point roughly halfway between Camp Eagle and the DMZ. It was early afternoon; we had just dropped off a load of arty ammo at a firebase in the mountains west of Camp Evans and were headed back to pick up another load. Soon we had cleared the mountains and were over coastal plains, less than five minutes from Evans. I relaxed a bit as I usually did when leaving the mountains. Just then, I heard a rapid thunk, thunk, thunk.

"Sir, we're taking hits!" yelled the flight engineer into his mouthpiece.

John, the AC, jerked up the thrust lever and yanked the cyclic over to the right which put the Chinook into a rapidly climbing right-hand turn. "Did you see where it came from? Anyone hurt?" The responses were all negative. "Chief, any noticeable damage?" John continued.

"I'm looking right now. So far it looks like three rounds came up through the floor amidships. No fluid leaks."

"We'll be on the ground in a couple minutes at Evans."

Oh man, first time taking hits. Scary. But it happened so quickly. Maybe not so scary. But we are still in the air. Who knows what vital part of the aircraft got hit? John, get this sucker on the ground! Fast! What if they start shooting again? I can still hear those rounds hitting our helicopter. My flight suit was wet with sweat.

After shutting down at Camp Evans, we went over every part of the aircraft. We'd been hit with three rounds of small arms fire, probably an AK-47. One round was embedded in a rotor blade, but the other two had exited the helicopter. Fortunately no critical systems had been damaged. We called our ops, and a maintenance officer was dispatched to our location on another Chinook to determine whether our aircraft was flyable. While we waited, I couldn't help but think about what had just happened. It seemed so personal to me:

someone on the ground had actually been shooting at me, probably hoping to down our aircraft, to kill me and my fellow crew members. Did he think about what that would mean to my parents, my friends? To him, I was no doubt just a nameless target of opportunity, no different than if one of our door gunners had seen him and hit him with a burst from an M-60 machine gun. All very impersonal, nothing more than a potential body count. So typical of war.

That evening at our ops meeting, the operations officer began with: "John Sharer took Dale Petersen out today and got his cherry." It was like I was being inducted into some exclusive club. After the fact, I was glad it had happened. I also hoped it was the last time.

I was actually able to go to chapel yesterday, the 16th of November. It was the first time in four weeks that I hadn't had to fly on a Sunday. In Nam it became very difficult to tell the difference between one day and the next. Each day was just like any other: another day in my 365-day "tour." I knew I could worship the Lord by myself any time I chose, but for the most part I didn't. I tried to pray some, but God seemed distant. I suppose that may have had something to do with me. But there was something about chapel that reconnected me to God and his Word. I didn't really understand it, but perhaps it was the presence of a chaplain, doing what I seemed incapable of doing: guiding a time of worship, digging into God's Word to find the comfort and strength it offered.

Most of our flying lately had taken us up near the "Z," in support of the ARVNs, carrying their ammo, water, food, and other supplies which were typical of most missions we flew. Once we flew some sorties of South Vietnamese troops. We'd squeezed ol' Marvin the ARVN real tight into the cargo compartment until we had a load of about seventy of them, double the number of G.I.s we'd typically carry per sortie.

Another time we flew in the opposite direction — southeast to Da Nang to pick up propaganda pamphlets for the psychological warfare guys at Camp Eagle. The pamphlets would soon be dropped over I Corp villages and hamlets. In fact, we had so many boxes of them that we made three round trips, which took the better part of a day. I saw one of the pamphlets. Since it was in Vietnamese I had no luck in deciphering it, although I did find out what part of it said: that Vietnamese could get paid some *piasters* (national currency) for turning in the names of VC sympathizers or for uncovering arms caches.

When I wasn't flying, I was busy with money. I was payroll officer for our company that month. To disburse the payroll, I established a couple different times when the G.I.s could line up to receive their pay. Each individual was required to come up to my desk, stand at attention, salute, and state his name. Then I would get the pay receipt, check it against each individual's ID card, and count out his pay in MPC, or military payment certificates, which we used in place of greenback dollars in Vietnam. All very traditional, very formal. Despite the orderliness, and despite the few make-up sessions I held to give even more opportunity for everyone to get paid, there was always someone who got missed because of heavy mission commitments, R & R, etc. They eventually got paid, but I didn't breathe a sigh of relief until all the money and records had balanced out, and I had turned back the records and remaining MPC into the finance office. I was liable for every cent of the more than $30,000 payroll, and I didn't take this lightly. It was even required that I have my loaded pistol close at hand whenever I had the payroll in my possession.

One sunny day — unusual since it had been mostly cloudy and rainy during November — when I had a day off from flying, I joined a couple of the other guys for a day of R & R in Da Nang. We caught the bus run (a daily, scheduled transportation service for G.I.s, rotated among the Chinook companies), which was easy since our company had the mission for that day. It felt very different flying in the back of a Chinook as a passenger instead of in my normal position in the cockpit. I was surprised to find that my stomach got quite queasy as we progressed toward Da Nang. There was a fair amount of turbulence, but then I'd experienced much more turbulence than that on a regular basis in the cockpit. The difference most likely was that in the cockpit I had a much better view out of the aircraft than I had in the back, where there were only a couple very small windows. And of course when I was in the cockpit I was focused on the mission being executed, while on that day I was just along for the ride. Fortunately I didn't up-chuck before we got off at China Beach. That would have been a hard one to live down.

China Beach was a strand of strikingly fine white sand on the South China Sea. It immediately felt like I was in a different world again, away from a war zone and in the middle of a seaside resort. There were several sunbathers and swimmers enjoying this tropical paradise seemingly so incongruous with its location in a war zone.

China Beach also had an officer's club renowned for its awesome cheeseburgers and French fries—two culinary delights I was starved for. The mere mention of them made me drool like a teething baby. I couldn't remember the last time I'd had a decent burger and fries … probably not since I'd left the world. When our lunch was served, we didn't know whether to slowly savor our delectable feast or to attack it. Attack mode won out, with gusto.

Afterward, we changed into swimsuits and headed for the beach. I went straight for the water and was surprised by how warm it was—almost the temperature of a pleasant bath. I stayed in the surf a long time, enjoying the tingling sensations of the warm water, trying to do a little body surfing, making my muscles pleasantly tired through a lot of swimming. Finally I reluctantly got out of the ocean and lay down on the beach. The sands were very soft and conformed to the curvature of my body. The sun was no longer high in the sky so it warmed my skin without frying it. I dozed off for a while. Soon we had to get back to the landing pad to catch our Chinook for the trip back to Camp Eagle — not the easiest thing to make ourselves do.

Recently Northern I Corps had become less of a placid setting. One Wednesday, units of the Fifth Mechanized Division — the only other American unit in our AO — ran into some very heavy contact with the NVA near the DMZ. In two days of fighting, there was a 200+ body count of NVA. The Fifth Mech guys suffered some relatively heavy casualties themselves. Several of us were just lounging around Wednesday when an urgent call came in to quickly launch six Chinooks from each company (eighteen in all). Crews were assigned to make up our six-aircraft complement. We all launched as soon as we could and flew to our staging area. There we loaded an entire battalion of troops onto the eighteen Chinooks. This battalion was part of a brigade that had been pulled back from the "Z" just a week before. All eighteen Chinooks flew in a loose trail formation up to Quang Tri which was the grunts' staging area. To lift an entire battalion in Chinooks at one time like this was unprecedented in Vietnam. This battalion together with the Fifth Mech units provided the firepower necessary to cause an NVA withdrawal, bringing a temporary lull in the action near the DMZ.

Chapter 14

O give thanks unto the Lord, for he is good:
for his mercy endureth for ever.

--Psalm 107:1 (KJV)

23 Nov. 69

Dear Donna,

The rain is dripping down as usual. I just got back from chapel. I really enjoyed it, especially since it was a Thanksgiving service. You know, when I stop and think about it, I've really got more to be thankful for than almost anybody else. When I look back, especially over the past couple years, it's really something how much I've been blessed. In addition to this, I have the most wonderful parents in the world. I have people who care about me and think of me. One of the greatest things, though, is that I have peace and am at ease in my heart...

Love, Pete

*　　　*　　　*

26 Nov. 69

Dear Donna,

...It's another rainy morning (so what else is new?). It's been raining steadily for the past three days. Our little creek has been rising, but I doubt if we'll get flooded again. The rain's not coming down nearly as hard as it did during the flood. There's another major phenomenon of weather occurring now. The temperature is going <u>down</u>. In fact, it's getting downright cold. We have to wear jackets most of the day lately. I even had to put an extra blanket on my bed. [I had asked my parents for an electric heater for Christmas because of the cold, and they had already sent it.] I used [it] a couple times. Don't you feel sorry for me? Actually, I think it's kinda fun. It's much nicer than dying of heat.

Tomorrow is Thanksgiving. We were told last night that we wouldn't have to fly then unless it's absolutely

113

necessary. It really might be almost like a holiday. Maybe we could be like the Pilgrims and Indians: we could invite some gooks over for turkey dinner! Okay, enough of my bright ideas...

Love, Dale

*　　*　　*

29 Nov. 69

Dear Donna,

Now that Thanksgiving is over, we're preparing for the big Christmas rush. I suppose that the Phu Bai Shopping Center and the Camp Eagle Mall will extend their open hours until 9 p.m. to accommodate the Christmas shoppers. Eagle International Airport is already feeling the crush of holiday travelers who are spending some time with friends. Screaming Eagle Boulevard is decorated with holly and strings of colorful Christmas lights. Oh, don't believe me, huh? Well, okay, I will stop with my fanciful dreams and dive back into reality.

They told us that we wouldn't have to fly on Thanksgiving unless it was absolutely necessary. You know, give us a holiday and all that. Well, I flew almost a full day. I didn't really mind, though. In fact, I was quite happy to do it, because we were carrying huge turkey dinners to isolated firebases most of the morning...

We did have ample time to eat our own turkey dinner. It was the finest meal I've eaten since I got to Nam. We had turkey with all the trimmings. Even had hot rolls and pumpkin pie, which is a real treat. Our mess hall was all decorated — looked real nice. Our company of about 200 personnel went through a dozen turkeys...

Love, Dale

Golf 2 Tango 4

Chapter 15

If I rise on the wings of the dawn,
if I settle on the far side of the
sea,
even there your hand will guide me,
your right hand will hold me fast.

--Psalm 139:9-10 (NIV)

early December 1969

"Mail call," I faintly heard a voice call out. I took my last swallow of coffee, put down my book, and headed for the O Club. There were several guys hanging around the pool table, waiting for the mail to get sorted. In addition to the usual batch of letters were several parcels. Christmas presents were already rolling in.

"If there are goodies in any of these packages, don't forget to share!" We all laughed, knowing each one of us would do everything he could to conceal such contents if he were the recipient.

I came away with a haul of a couple letters, one from Donna and one from my folks, and a couple of packages. I never lost the thrill of having mail with my name on it. Everything became secondary to savoring my mail. I enjoyed the privacy of my hootch on many occasions, but especially when I had mail to open and read. I slowly read both letters, then reread them a couple more times. Soon it was time to deal with the packages, both from Donna. Both boxes opened up to Christmas wrapping.

Okay, now what do I do? I asked myself as I started examining the presents. *I probably should wait till Christmas, but that's a long time from now.*

Then I noticed that one of the packages was marked: "Do not wait until Christmas to open."

I'm sure that's meant for both packages, I tried to convince myself. My moral dilemma lasted about a split second before I tore the paper off the unmarked package. Inside I beheld a treasure of cookies and other goodies. My eyes must have been directly connected to my salivary glands as my mouth filled with moisture. I grabbed three or four cookies and stuffed them in my mouth as fast as I could, then grabbed another three for more leisurely consumption. *See? No way I should've waited for Christmas,* I justified to myself. *Plus, I'll share some with Phil when he gets in.*

Then I turned my attention to the other package, the one with the note not to wait. I opened it, and much to my surprise there was a Christmas tree! A couple of the guys had small trees sent from home, but I'd just figured I would have to do without this year. A Christmas tree had always been one of those singular symbols that heralded the Christmas season for me. I loved the shape, the color, the ornaments, the lights. It always made for such a festive air, pointing to family gatherings, carols, gifts, snow, familial warmth, the church Christmas program, the manger. I lifted the tree out of the box — it was all of twelve to eighteen inches tall, accompanied by its own stand and a package of ornaments. It didn't take me long to decorate it and find the perfect place to display it on our piece of plywood that resembled a table/desk. That little artificial tree was one of the best Christmas presents I could ever remember. I sat back and enjoyed the new cheery atmosphere of our hootch. AFVN was playing some Christmas songs. I slowly munched a cookie and smiled.

The next morning we were headed up to the "Z" at daybreak. Although it wasn't raining at the moment, there were low scudding clouds driven by a rather stiff wind. It looked bleak and felt somewhat chilly. The ceiling (cloud level) was too low to maintain our usual fifteen-hundred-foot AGL. We followed Highway One between Hue and Quang Tri—called "the Street Without Joy" by the French many years ago—as we typically did. We would be flying our usual re-supply loads to the extent that we were able in view of the weather.

After a morning of sorties and attempted sorties, we shut down for some lunch: C-rations as usual. I was happy with the ham and eggs. I used my tin of a cheese whiz-like substance to enhance the ham and eggs a little. Gourmet lunch at that.

After we performed a quick aircraft inspection, we cranked up and were airborne again. The AC was flying this sortie and picked up a load of PSP and other construction materials destined for a firebase in the nearby mountains. The ceiling seemed to be lowering and thickening. It was rainy and foggy, the visibility deteriorating. As we were approaching the firebase, we were right at cloud level—so close it seemed like I could reach up out my window and touch those puffs of grey. In another split second, we went inadvertent IFR, into the soup. The AC starting pulling up, and the next thing I knew he had punched off the load.

"Hey, we just lost our load," said the flight engineer.

"You just lost your load, Varsity," the pathfinder seconded over the radio.

My skin felt clammy and my body shivered involuntarily. I fought a wave of panic. We were definitely in the soup, absolutely in the clouds with no ground reference whatsoever. We appeared to be losing airspeed and were rolling slightly. Then to top it off: "I've got vertigo," said the AC.

I jumped on the controls. "I got it."

I tried to focus only on the instruments. My body was telling me that we were rolling to the left, but the instruments were telling me we were rolling the other direction. I fought the feeling in my body. *Believe your instruments, believe your instruments!* I said to myself, just like they taught us in flight school. It was chilly but I was sweating profusely. *Don't panic,* I reminded myself. I got the attitude indicator level, cross-referenced that with the turn and slip indicator, and held it there to make sure the aircraft was stabilized. I fought the feeling in my body that told me we were still rolling. A wave of nausea was rising in my gut. I increased our airspeed and made sure we were climbing. When the aircraft was stabilized at a level attitude, good airspeed and proper climb rate, I started a gradual left turn to keep us from going too far north or west. I had very little instrument flying experience outside of my time in flight school, and I was struggling to keep my focus on the instruments rather than the feelings in my body. Abject fear was lurking much too close. In what seemed like an eternity but was really only a couple minutes, we broke out of the clouds and into the sunlight. Seldom have I seen such a glorious sight. All of a sudden we had references again—the sky, the mountaintops, the clouds below us. The dissonance between body and instruments was gone.

"I got it," said the AC.

"You got it." My chest was pounding and my muscles were tensed. I sat back and tried to relax. I lit a cigarette and began to settle down. The AC brought the aircraft to an easterly heading, away from the mountains. We got a vector from Quang Tri air traffic control to let us down through the clouds. The AC was intent on flying the aircraft through the soup this time. As we entered the clouds, I focused on the instruments as if I were flying, just in case anything happened again. This time the AC had no problems. I felt relief as we broke out of the clouds and saw the coastal plains again.

The AC called ops and told them we were coming in since the weather had just gotten too bad for any more sorties. After we had landed in the Locker Room, I thought he might want to talk a little about what had happened, but he said nary a word. He would have to go report the lost load. I guessed that he was embarrassed, but as I thought about it, I didn't think he needed to be. Getting vertigo as a result of an inadvertent IFR incident was not an unheard of occurrence. We used to get it pounded into our heads in flight school: if you are going to encounter IFR flying, make sure you do it in a planned manner under the supervision of air traffic control. And in retrospect, I'm glad he punched off that load. The last thing we needed when we went into the soup, when we were trying to stabilize the aircraft, was to have a load like that oscillating under us. Besides, it was building materials, not ammo or an artillery piece.

That night as I lay on my bunk, trying to coax the fog of sleep to bless me with its presence, my mind wandered back over the past couple days. Yesterday I was in the Christmas spirit, enjoying gifts from home and decorating my living quarters like Christmases past, reflecting on the life-giving joy of the Advent. And today, in stark contrast, overwhelming fear was dominant as I literally fought a death struggle with the aircraft and myself. I simply couldn't grasp how one day could exist alongside the other.

Chapter 16

*For unto us a child is born, unto us a
son is given:
and the government shall be upon his
shoulder:
and his name shall be called
Wonderful, Counsellor,
The mighty God, The everlasting
Father, The Prince of Peace.*

--Isaiah 9:6 (KJV)

10 Dec. 69

Dear Donna,

Guess what! Even I am starting to get into the Christmas spirit. The radio is playing Christmas songs every once in awhile. My Christmas tree (from a certain sweet young thing) is all beautifully decorated which cheers up the room 110%. You couldn't have picked a better gift, and once again I want to thank you for it. Oh, those scrumptious goodies of yours are mostly calories on my waistline...

I've been getting lax on letter-writing lately again. Sorry. We've been having a busy few days lately. The weather broke somewhat so we were flying our little tails off. We've been flying a lot of support for the ARVNs lately: carrying them water, food, and artillery ammo. We've also been carrying a lot of U.S. troops around. They've been conducting a lot of sweeps around the coastal plains near here. We sorta hopscotch them from one location to another. This gives them the element of surprise.

Two days ago, Camp Eagle had its first rocket attack in over two months. It was in broad daylight, just before supper time. I was goofing around outside when I heard a loud ka-boom! on our flight line. There were two more explosions not more than 100 yards from our living area. Those were the first rockets we've absorbed in our company area since I got here. Yup, it made me jump. No one got hurt, but two of our ships were pretty badly blasted with shrapnel...

Love, Dale

*　　*　　*

18 Dec. 69

Dear Donna,

I'm late with a letter again. I guess it's just all this hustle and bustle of the holiday season...No, I have been terribly busy. Trying to do too many things at once. A couple days ago I became physically and mentally exhausted. I was in bed for a couple days with headaches and fever. I drank lots of orange juice, though, so I'm fine now...

That description of what we could do together if I was there now was beautiful. You picked out the things that I love most about Christmas: shopping downtown with all its decorations, decorating the tree, wrapping presents, sitting in front of the fire...I love Christmas and descriptions like you gave. I only wish it were a reality instead of a dream...

Hey, did I tell you that Camp Eagle is supposed to be one of the stops on Bob Hope's Christmas tour? I sure hope it's not just a rumor...What's more, two ships from our company have been selected to carry his troupe and some of their equipment around. The real catcher is that I've been selected on one of the crews. Can't you just see me flying Bob Hope and a bevy of voluptuous young things around? I sure could see it. I'll let you know what progresses.

...I got a very nice card from your folks. I really appreciate sweet little remembrances like that: it's good to know you're not forgotten. I'm actually quite flattered getting a greeting from your folks.

Since it'll be about Christmas when you get this, I'll wish you a very special merry Christmas and nothing but the best for such a sweet young thing as you. Never forget that you are in my thoughts as always.

Much love, Dale

*   *   *

19 Dec. 69

Dear Donna,

...Do you realize that one week from now all the stores will be having their post-Christmas sales? ...The date I'm really looking forward to is 24 July 1970. Sounds an awful long way off yet, right? Oh well, if five months went by okay, no reason why I can't hack seven more. I just wish so badly that I could be in the States, playing like a carefree kid in the snow... No, I'm not really down and homesick tonight, just wishing, you know?

Not much happening around here. The weather is the same, only the visibility is worse each day and the clouds come lower. The rain continues to fall. I did fly to Da Nang yesterday – all the way through the "soup." That instrument flying is rather tricky. We did break out of the clouds at 8,000 feet on the way to Da Nang. It was the most breathtakingly beautiful sight I've seen in a long time. There we were on top of solid clouds, nothing but blue sky above us and the sun shining brightly. It was an all-new beautiful world, something I would never have witnessed if my dear Lord hadn't helped me to be a pilot. I can never be thankful enough for this. That mystical beauty up there is an unmatched experience for me. It was the complete peace of the scene which awe-struck me so...

I guess I'd better get to bed. I'll try to dream pleasant dreams. I've had pretty fitful nights the last few nights...

Much love, Dale

*   *   *

21 Dec. 69

Dear Donna,

Here it is the end of another Sunday and am I ever tired. The weather broke yesterday and today so we've been flying our little tails off from first light till after dark. In these past two days I've gotten 22 flying hours, and my hind quarters can really tell it from sitting in the cockpit all day... Needless to say, I didn't get to chapel today. I really miss it, but when the weather breaks, we have to fly all we can.

...We've been hauling in much needed supplies (ammo, food, etc.) to most of the firebases around here. [T]hey've been socked in for quite a few days and have been getting critically short of supplies. Most of the firebases we hauled into were up on the "Z." It sure was good to fly again when you could see something, [and see] where you were going. The wind really came up, though, setting up almost intolerable turbulence in the mountains. You get terrific buffeting coming in on final approach to those pinnacles. Sometimes it's hard to even control the aircraft. Sounds like a good sob story, huh?

...Did I ever tell you about all the mail I've been getting recently? My name was in the Banner *[periodical of the* Christian Reformed Church] *and also in the* Seattle Times' *Christmas Mailing List, so I've been getting all kinds of cards from people I've never known before. Most of them have been girls... very interesting! I've also been getting a few cards from a certain fan club in Mich[igan]. Seems that the president is a young lady by the name of Donna Steffens. Do you know anything about that? ...*

Much love, Dale

Chapter 17

Glory to God in the highest,
And on earth peace, good will toward
men.

--Luke 2:14 (KJV)

Platte, South Dakota
Christmas Eve, circa 1958

Snow crunched under my rubber boots as I walked along the streets. "If the snow crunches when you walk, you know it's extra cold," Dad would often say. I had put on double gloves, double jeans, and double socks. I had two heavy shirts under my parka, and the hood was cinched tight over my head. With all of that on, my fingers and toes were still getting very cold, and I could hardly feel my nose. I would need to stop at one of my customers' to warm up. I selected the elderly De Haan's house because it was about halfway through my paper route. That's where I usually stopped anyway, and they'd be expecting me. I knocked at their door and sweet old Mrs. De Haan answered a moment later.

"May I come in and warm up?" I asked, at the same time she was saying, "Come in, come in! It's cold out there." I took off my gloves, coat, boots and shoes. They already had a chair for me sitting by a heat register on which I could put my feet.

"I thought you might be early since the Christmas program is tonight," said Mr. De Haan as he sat at the kitchen table. "Do you have to say a piece in it?"

I nodded. "I've been going over it while I've been delivering the newspapers. I don't want to make a mistake."

I had already handed him his paper and he was eagerly turning to the comics section. In less than a minute he was chuckling. "I love that Blondie. She's my girlfriend."

Mrs. De Haan brought me my usual cup of hot milk she'd just heated on the stove and a small plate of cookies. "Here, this will warm you up."

The hot milk felt so pleasantly warm as it made its way down to my stomach. The furnace was running almost continuously, so my feet were getting an ample supply of heat. My toes and fingers started to tingle and then had a burning sensation. It didn't take too long for the burning to go away and for toes and fingers to feel just normal again. I watched as Mrs. De Haan checked their supper on the stove and Mr. De Haan finished the comic section. They always seemed so happy.

I started putting on my winter clothes again. "Did you warm up enough?"

"I sure did. Thanks for letting me warm up and for the hot milk. And those cookies sure were good."

"You be sure to stop by anytime."

I stepped outside. The cold air made me gasp momentarily. Then I was on my way. In places where the sidewalk hadn't been shoveled, I struggled to get through the snowdrifts, sometimes sinking in beyond my knees. My newspaper bag dragged along on top of the snow. It was hard work, but all I was aware of was my excitement that the snowstorm meant we would have a white Christmas. The muffling blanket of snow added to the quiet of the neighborhoods. Even the sound of a passing car was muted as its tires swished through the snow. And there were signs of Christmas everywhere. Most houses had decorated Christmas trees with multi-colored lights looking out from a prominent window. A few people had even put lights on the outside of their houses. But nothing could top the thrill of looking down Main Street: long strings of Christmas lights zigzagging across the street from light pole to light pole, a kaleidoscope of light and color.

I looked up into the night sky with its dazzling brilliance of stars, and the Milky Way spreading out over the infinite deep of the heavens. As usual I located the Big Dipper, then the North Star at the end of the Little Dipper's handle. All seemed right with my world. It was one of my favorite times of the year.

As I neared the end of my route, I asked one of my customers if I could use their phone. "Dad," I said into the mouthpiece, "I'm almost done. Please come and pick me up."

"Okay, I'm leaving now. I'll pick you up at the end of your route." This had become a routine on bitterly cold evenings, especially since my route ended up on the north side of town, several blocks from home.

In just a short while I saw the car coming. As I got in I could feel the warmth of the car heater as the fan blew the warm air throughout the interior. "Don called right after you did and we have to go get him now," Dad said. A couple minutes later, as we pulled over into the trackless snow on the side of the road to pick up Don, Dad said, "Shoot, I think we got stuck." Sure enough, the car just spun its back wheels. I knew the snow shovel was in the trunk—Dad would never drive on a night like this without it. He quickly shoveled snow out from underneath the car and around the wheels. "Okay, boys, you push." In no time we were out on the street again and headed for home.

As we got out of the car at home, I heard Christmas carols playing over loudspeakers placed in the church belfry. Our home was the parsonage, right next to the church. "Hey, Dad, I like the Christmas music. I bet people can hear it halfway across town."

"Did you stay warm?" Mom asked as we came in the door.

"Oh, man, it's cold out there. Yeah, I warmed up at the De Haan's. Dad, what temp is it?"

He opened the inside window over the kitchen sink so he could rub the frost off the storm window and see the thermometer. "It's five below." That was met with a chorus of "ooohs!"

"Okay, everyone wash their hands. It's supper time." We ate supper more quickly than usual because we needed to get ready for the Christmas program.

In spite of the weather, church was as full as usual. Although the congregation was normally very solemn for worship services, they always seemed to have received special dispensation to smile and even chat softly before the Christmas program. There was the usual chaos of kids finding their seats, getting in the right order. We'd practiced this all several times, but with such a gaggle of kids, it always happened this way. Some of the guys who were the normal hair-pullers and pinchers had to be much more circumspect that night since the eyes of hundreds of parents and other church members were upon us.

The program got underway pretty much on time. Dad gave the invocation as he did for regular worship services and any special program. He would give the benediction as well, but no sermon that night. I was secretly thankful for that. The sermon would come tomorrow morning. The program had its usual variety of songs sung by different age groups, a changing tableau on the platform in front of the sanctuary, and many short speaking parts (or "pieces" as some called them), all moving the story line forward to the stable with its manger in Bethlehem. I always did like the Christmas story, in fact I was astounded by it—that God would come to Earth as a baby just because he loved us so much. Sometimes it was so hard to imagine something so wonderful could happen that I would wonder if it really did happen. I didn't dare tell anyone that. And I mostly believed it anyway. I just wished I didn't have a piece to worry about so I could just for once sit back, relaxed, and watch the story unfold. At least if I had to have a piece, why couldn't it be in the beginning of the program so I could get it over with? But tonight it came later.

Some things never changed in the Christmas program, especially when it was the youngest kids' turns. The congregation always seemed to save the biggest smiles for them. And when the inevitable flub occurred, I could detect a murmur of laughter. But of course there was always an adult with the script for the whole program in his or her lap, who could prompt the participants with the correct words. Still, at age ten, there's no way you wanted to have to be prompted.

I could tell it was nearly my turn. I ran through my piece in my head quickly one last time. Only two more parts before mine ... then one ... my turn. I stood up. I could feel a lot of eyes on me, but I said as loud as I could without shouting: "Peace I leave with you, my peace I give unto you: not as the world giveth, give I unto you. Let not your heart be troubled, neither let it be afraid. John 14:27" (KJV). Relief flooded my insides. I had done it. I sat down.

Soon it was over. We kids were dismissed first, while the adults had to wait. We knew why. As we went into the foyer, each of us got a bag of candy and an orange. Even though I didn't like most of the hard candy that was in the bag, I knew it would also contain some chocolate, which enhanced the little bag's value. And although I didn't eat oranges very often, the fact that the one in this bag was a special gift at Christmas meant I always ate that one.

My friends and I gathered in our usual corner in the church basement. Most of the guys would be opening their Christmas presents as soon as they got home that evening. I was shocked when one guy said they would open theirs on Christmas morning. I didn't think anyone would ever do that—my parents had always indicated that Christmas day was a sacred day, a day for going to church, not for secular activities like opening Christmas gifts. I was always a little embarrassed that our family opened our gifts on the evening of December 23. I think Mom and Dad thought Christmas Eve was too busy an evening, and after the program it was about bedtime for my little brothers.

When I got home, I went into the living room and sat by the Christmas tree. My stash of Christmas gifts lay in a small pile where I had left them after I'd opened them the previous night. I picked each up and looked it over. My eager pre-Christmas anticipation had not been dashed—I got a pleasant surprise or two and also a couple things that had been high on my wish list, especially thrilling was a model airplane. I put down my gifts, looked at the tree for awhile, and wished the season would never end.

*   *   *

25 December 1969

I slowly came out of a deep sleep. Maybe my body and mind had relaxed a little more last night because we were in the middle of a Christmas cease-fire. Ah yes, peace on earth and goodwill to everyone.

But then I realized that it was darker than it should be, and I could hear dripping on the roof. I poked my head out the door and my heart about stopped. The visibility was so bad that I couldn't even see the flight line which was virtually next door to our hootches. Today was Christmas day, and it was also the day of the big Bob Hope Christmas Show here at Camp Eagle. We had found out just a few days ago that the rumors were true and the show was actually going to happen. But as I looked at the weather, I was sure we wouldn't be able to fly and the show would be cancelled.

Bob Hope and his troupe had spent the night on the aircraft carrier USS Ranger, which was stationed about thirty miles east of Hue on the South China Sea. Chinooks from our company and the other 159th companies had been assigned to carry the cast, as well as equipment and other stage materials. The bird I was on had been designated the stand-by ship, so we would fly only if someone ran into mechanical trouble. But if the weather didn't improve some, no one would be going, and there would be no show. My morale factor was rapidly sinking.

All the crews had been waiting around for a couple hours when, quite suddenly, the weather lifted. The order came down to go, and the primary birds for the Bob Hope mission lifted off. That meant my stand-by crew would not, and I had probably missed out on my chance to fly Bob Hope. There was another big mission that day—many Chinooks and Hueys would be ferrying

G.I.s from far-flung firebases and other outlying base camps to Camp Eagle for the show. However, the crew to which I was assigned had to remain on stand-by for the Hope mission in case one of our primary aircraft developed mechanical problems en route.

Within the hour, the skies began to fill with inbound helicopters. The Locker Room was one of the designated landing areas for this mission. A couple of other guys and I became impromptu pathfinders and did some sector air traffic control with a PRC-25 portable radio. A few deuce and a half (2½-ton) trucks waited nearby to take G.I.s from our landing pad to the outdoor theater for the show. The guys getting off the helicopters were in a noticeably festive mood. There was a lot of laughing, joking and good-natured elbowing going on. I suppose any change of scenery was welcome to these guys who had been in remote locations for so long, and to be able to see the Bob Hope show live was definitely the cherry on top of the sundae.

The troop ferrying continued for at least a couple hours. We got word that all the Chinooks had made it to the USS Ranger and were now inbound. I felt a strong wave of disappointment—no high profile mission for me today. I had gotten close to it, but that was all. In a way, I wished I hadn't even been on stand-by: that way I might not have felt such a sense of loss when it didn't happen. And since I'd been on stand-by, I hadn't even gotten to be a part of the ferry mission, which would have been very satisfying. I was feeling rather sorry for myself.

With less than half an hour to go before showtime, we headed out for the show venue. Since the stand-by crew was considered part of the Hope mission, we got reserved seats up front. As we approached the outdoor theater and got our first glimpse of it, I was stunned by the sea of people. There were literally thousands— probably close to fifteen thousand in all—sitting on a shallow hill side, a natural amphitheater within Camp Eagle. One of my first thoughts was: I sure hope Charlie is observing the ceasefire and doesn't start lobbing mortars and rockets in here. It might have been a holiday, but a soldier's innate sense of threat doesn't rest easily.

The show was mesmerizing for me—even the stupid jokes Bob Hope read from his huge cue cards. Connie Stevens sang. Ann Charney worked her way through a sensual dance routine as fifteen thousand G.I.s went out of their minds. The Goldiggers from TV's Dean Martin Show did a couple of dance numbers. One of the best parts of the program was when Neil Armstrong came out: he got a long, loud standing ovation. It gave me shivers up my spine. I remembered back to the previous July when he had first set foot on the moon, five days before I had left home for Vietnam. The most touching part was the last number of the program, when we all sang "Silent Night" together. Some guys had tears in their eyes.

In the mess hall that day we had an incredible feast almost identical to Thanksgiving. Later that evening a few of us sat around, just talking. Then we started singing Christmas carols. It was all quite spontaneous, quietly joyous yet somber. As we sang "Silent Night," some of us sang in parts. As I went through the verses of that hauntingly beautiful song, it got more and more difficult to sing well. I thought maybe our a cappella rendition had started out too low and I couldn't hit all the bass notes, but then I noticed that my throat was thickening quite a bit. I stopped for awhile, tried to make my body stop shaking, and closed my eyes.

Chapter 18

*Would it turn out well if [God]
examined you?
Could you deceive him as you deceived
men?*

--Job 13:9 (NIV)

26 December 1969

Christmas of 1969 was past, which meant the next time I celebrated it I'd be back in the good ol' USA. I was getting close to the halfway point of my tour, and I was starting to feel like an experienced Chinook driver. Within the next month, I would probably be made an aircraft commander. I really wanted to be an AC, but at the same time the thought made me nervous and a little scared. No longer would I be able to rely on someone else to fly the really difficult scenarios or to make the decisions for our aircraft—that would be me instead.

Later in the afternoon several of us were sitting around, chewing the fat like we often did. This time the primary subject was all about flying the Bob Hope cast the previous day from the USS Ranger to Camp Eagle. The guys on that mission regaled us with many of the details. It was the coolest of missions, and they had had a great time with it. It was very different from the kind of flying we normally did. The more they talked about it, the more disappointed I was that I hadn't been able to be a part of it. But outwardly I laughed and nodded agreeably like the rest of the guys.

The flight out to the USS Ranger had been uneventful, but landing on its deck was a new kind of experience. The aircraft carrier was of course moving forward but was also pitching somewhat on the sea. One guy told us what this had been like for him.

"The flight engineer was trying to help me out by describing the deck's motion. I just hovered over it for awhile trying to figure out how I'd put it down. Finally, when I figured I knew at least a little bit about the carrier's rhythm, I just planted it on the deck. We hit pretty hard, but we were down okay."

All the play-by-plays spun out vividly in my head, as I re-lived the experience with the men. As it turned out, the weather delay had messed up the order: which bird would be out at the Ranger when, and who was to carry what. The guys from Varsity had originally been slated to carry equipment, but when they landed on the carrier, all that was left to carry was the cast and Bob Hope himself. The guys shook hands with him, and he'd asked if he could sit on the jump seat. The jump seat is in the companionway which goes between the cockpit and the cargo area. Sitting there, he would be right behind the pilots and could see what they were doing. He also had his trademark golf club with him, which he was waving around while he talked, using it as a pointer; the guys agreed to his request, silently hoping he wouldn't be swinging that club around inside the helicopter.

After they landed at Camp Eagle, they had gotten to talk with Hope and some of the cast for a few minutes, including Connie Stevens, Ann Charney, Neil Armstrong, and Miss World. The stars were all very friendly and gracious. Then the cast had to get ready for the show, and the mission was over. Our guys tried to take an "aw, shucks" attitude about rubbing elbows with celebrities, but they had clearly enjoyed it. The rest of us tried not to show our envy too much.

What a great story! They really had something to tell their grandchildren about. I wanted it to be my story, too. In fact, a thought began percolating in my mind—I *could* make it my story. I could tell my family and friends back home, and they wouldn't know any better. It would be harmless, and everyone would think I was extra cool. Guys did it all the time, anyway, or so I guessed. They might embellish an action, more or less, when telling a "war story." Besides, the telling of war stories like this was as old as warfare itself, I was sure. So I decided to do it. That evening I wrote Donna, and the story of flying the Bob Hope cast became my story. I also wrote Mom and Dad about "my" mission on Christmas Day. I wasn't too concerned about it at the time; after all, like I said, it was just a war story, just an embellishment. Another common word for it hadn't yet risen to a level of consciousness in my mind—a lie.

The next day I began feeling a bit uneasy about it—I started having second thoughts. But it was too late because the mail had been picked up already, and the letters to the world were on their way. "Aw, forget about it," I told myself. "This will be fun, and I'll get a lot of attention—maybe even adoration."

In a couple of weeks, I got a response back from Donna, the response I had been looking for. But there wasn't a lot of satisfaction in it. A few days later I got my parents' response, and it was quite a bit more than I had expected. The letter included a clipping from the Lynden, Washington weekly newspaper. It wasn't a big article, just a couple paragraphs, but the two-word headline said it all: "Flies Hope." In addition to my "war story," the article did include some accurate information: Dad had told the reporter about the relief supplies we'd flown into some of the villages during the floods of October, which made the second paragraph of the story. But the lie about Bob Hope was certainly most prominent, positioned right in the first paragraph.

I was sick. I didn't think it was cool at all anymore. I just wanted the whole thing to be gone, as if it had never happened. I just had to set things straight somehow, but I didn't know how; it was just too late. I'd simply have to come clean ... but that would devastate my parents. And I sure wouldn't be very cool in Donna's eyes anymore. No telling what direction our relationship would turn after that. I decided to keep my mouth shut.

When I first came to Vietnam, one of my biggest concerns was that I not be a coward. Halfway through my tour, I had become one.

Chapter 19

You are my friends…

--John 15:14 (NIV)

31 December 1969

I was watching my steak closely as it seared on our barbecue grill. With a lot of guys trying to cook their steaks, there was quite a bit of jockeying for position. It was all good-natured fun. I think we were at our most relaxed and carefree at our cookouts. I'm not sure why that was the case—perhaps it was a reminder of special times back home. Anyway, the camaraderie was something I treasured.

I was getting to know some of the guys quite well now that we'd had several months together. However, there was always someone leaving as the various one-year tours came to an end, and of course there were always replacements being introduced to the company. The good-byes were not so easy, but they were just a part of the rhythm of life at Camp Eagle. And each time I met a new guy, I was sure it would take a long time to get to know him. Yet usually after a few short weeks, the newbie seemed to fit right in.

I thought of home a lot, but it seemed largely like a dream world. That was kind of weird since I had a lot of contact with it, via significant amounts of mail from Donna, my parents, and others. But Camp Eagle and Northern I Corps were the reality that constituted my life for the time being. That was where I ate, slept, went to "work," and carried on my face-to-face social interactions. I guess the dream aspect of that world was due to the fact that Sumas, Washington was totally incongruous with Vietnam. There was no way I could physically bridge the chasm between the two, and even more significantly, no way to bridge the internal gap between the life I lived back home with my life here. When I thought of home, it was like a distant memory that was simply not tangible.

After stuffing ourselves with all the good food at our New Year's Eve celebration, several of us retired to Gork Outdoor Theater to watch that evening's flick. We could never know what we were going to get—it might be a recent first-run movie, or it could be some obscure film from celluloid history no one had ever heard of before. Our feature for that evening fell into the latter category: it was a British musical called "Half A Sixpence" starring Tommy Steele. ...Huh? Obviously we were pretty desperate since we were willing to sit through that. Actually, when it was over with, I had to admit it was a rather happy, carefree-type movie which kind of made me feel good.

When midnight came, we didn't need to be informed. It seemed like everyone on the bunker line, around the entire perimeter, was shooting off flares. The sky was filled with white, red, and green flares. Some of us shot off pencil flares from our survival vests. It was quite a sight, although I don't know how much the higher-ups appreciated it. Regardless, it felt like a festive welcome to a new year and a new decade. 1970—this was the year I'd get to go home.

Dale H. Petersen

*   *   *

5 Jan. 70

Dear Donna,

Do you realize that almost one week of 1970 is already past history?...

By the way, what was the matter with the U. of Mich. in the Rose Bowl, letting USC beat them that way?...[Yes,] I did get to listen to the Bowl games on the radio which I really liked. Next year, though, I'm going to watch them. I tell ya, that's what's <u>really</u> bad over here: I had to miss a whole season of football. Can you think of anything worse than that?

...Yesterday I didn't get to chapel because I was flying all day. We were pulling out a large firebase in the mountains. I guess those guys were getting tired of being socked in the clouds for long periods of time, so we moved them to the lowlands. It was one of the few permanent firebases [...]left in the mountains during this monsoon season. I imagine that when the dry season starts in a couple months, we'll be putting in firebases from Da Nang to the DMZ and from the coast to the Laotian border...

...Hope everything is fine with you and that you are taking care. Pray for happiness and peace in this new decade.

Much love, Dale

*   *   *

11 Jan 70

Dear Donna,

...The weather has turned <u>cold</u> again. I flew some today, but when I was on the ground, I got into my room which is warmed by my electric heater. The rain and drizzle continue to fall...[Western] Washington has an arid climate compared to

the Vietnam monsoon season. We've been having rain ever since the monsoons started with a bang in Oct. with the floods. I think I'd be stretching it if I said we've had ten sunny days since Oct. One thing I can't overlook, though, is that it's been real nice for sleeping…

Much love, Dale

Chapter 20

*I know that there is nothing better
for men
than to be happy and do good while
they live.*

--Ecclesiastes 3:12 (NIV)

17 January 1970

I had been assigned the stand-by bird today, so we'd be going through our normal pre-flight inspection. We would even crank up and bring both engines on line to make sure there were no problems. But after that the aircraft would be shut down and our crew would wait throughout the day to see if we had to launch or not. Generally, the stand-by aircraft was only used if one of the company's Chinooks that had been assigned to fly that day couldn't launch for some reason. In addition, if a new mission came down that one of the airborne crews couldn't handle, that mission would be given to the stand-by helicopter.

This day was much more momentous than just being on stand-by, though. A single thought stood front and center in my brain: "*I*" had the stand-by bird today. This was to be my first official day as an aircraft commander. I had taken a check ride the day before and passed it, and therefore had been designated as an AC. Of course, that meant I would be ultimately responsible for the safety of my aircraft and crew, and would be the one responsible for the satisfactory completion of all assigned missions. Every time that thought entered my mind, I noticed an involuntary shiver go down my spine.

Even though it made me a bit nervous to think of having so much responsibility, I had already flown a few days as "pilot-in-charge," which was a de facto AC. Those times of being in charge helped to mitigate my fears and gave me some confidence that I was in fact up to the task of being an AC. In the past few weeks we'd had several aircraft commanders complete their tours and rotate back out to the world. All of a sudden Varsity had become a bit lean when it came to experienced pilots. So "pilot-in-charge" had become my temporary designation until I could get a check ride. My roomie Phil had been in the same boat.

Approximately one week before, my first day of flying as "pilot-in-charge" had begun without ceremony. When I was awakened by the ops clerk that morning, I had no reason to suspect I'd be flying without an AC. But when he told me I'd be flying with George Mason, I knew something had changed in my status. George had two months and many flying hours less experience than I did. And not that it mattered, but George was even younger than I was—he'd barely turned twenty. At breakfast, the ops officer, Captain Dave Magers, talked to me briefly about it: "We gotta go with experience, and you and Phil and me are next in line." Dave had come in country the same time Phil and I had. He tried to reassure me: "You can do it, Pete."

My pre-flight inspection took somewhat longer and was just a bit more thorough than usual that morning. It felt very strange as I settled into the left seat for the first time. Seeing George, the "Okie from Muskogee" (mostly we called him Little George to distinguish him from his older and more portly namesake who went by Big George) next to me in the right-hand seat only added to the "new and different" atmosphere, because we'd never flown together before this day.

"Okay, George, it's you and me today. Let's see if we can get this done and get back okay."

Our first mission was up near the "Z," and by the time we'd flown the half hour or so to get there, I was already feeling less stressed. We had a very unique mission, or at least new to us—we would be spraying defoliants around a firebase. We landed at a staging area in Quang Tri and shut down. We were met by a team who fitted our aircraft with spray bars that stuck out on either side from underneath the helicopter. One of their chemical guys joined us for the mission to ensure the defoliants got where they were supposed to. We cranked up again and were soon airborne with our chemicals and temporary appendage hanging from our aircraft.

The firebase was on the coastal plains that lay within a couple miles of the DMZ. From the perimeter outward all we could see were tall grass and heavy underbrush. From our viewpoint I could understand why they'd want this area defoliated: it looked like the bad guys could easily get right up to the wire without being detected. We flew around that firebase spraying chemicals for a couple hours or so. It was a fun kind of flying—we had to go low-level and circle the base time and again. It had the feel of doing laps around a racetrack. I didn't know what chemicals we were spraying, but I was glad we didn't get any on us.

Right across the DMZ was a large NVA camp. We could see a big red flag waving above it. For some reason our artillery or planes weren't allowed to shoot at it. I guessed that was because of last year's bombing halt over the North. And as far as I knew, that camp never fired south across the DMZ either. I suppose they knew they'd get plenty of return fire if they did. It was kind of a weird sight seeing that big flag so close to us.

The day of my defoliation mission, and the next few days as "pilot-in-charge," passed without incident. All the aircraft had launched for their morning missions, so we were still in a stand-by mode. After breakfast I did some reading, then chatted with a couple guys over coffee.

The next thing I knew, I heard my name being called. Dave found me and said, "Hey, Pete, you gotta launch right away. We got a mission from battalion ops. They need a Super-C." That day I had been assigned a Super-C, a particular model of a Chinook. The Army was doing a modification to the old C models, primarily a re-engine program including beefed-up transmissions and drive train to increase the lift capability substantially. "A truck overturned by a bridge over the Perfume River in Hue and a couple G.I.s are trapped inside. They need you to lift it so they can get the guys out."

I found Tom Hirschler, my pilot, in his hootch and told him what was going on. "Go ahead and get the aircraft started while I get briefed in ops," I told him. Normally we didn't start our engines without both pilots in their seats, but given the nature of the mission, we needed to do everything we could to shorten our response time.

It didn't take me long to get the necessary radio frequencies for our ground contacts and also the location of the accident. By the time I got back to the aircraft, Tom was already well into his engine start sequence. "Go ahead and fly to Hue while I make a couple radio calls," I said. After I made the necessary contacts, I briefed Tom and the crew on the details as I knew them. The flight engineer started connecting several cargo straps together, then reached down and connected them to the cargo hook.

As we approached the bridge, we could see the five-ton truck overturned beside it, almost in the river. Apparently it had swerved to avoid a bicyclist. There was a huge crowd gathered on and around the bridge, watching what was going on. The accident site was near several tall trees, around one hundred feet high. We had to hover above them and drop the connected cargo straps to the truck. The cab of the truck needed to be lifted so rescuers could get the two guys out who were pinned inside and underneath. The difficulty was holding our high hover. Since we were so far off the ground, the only good reference points we had were the tops of trees which were blowing because of our rotor wash. If we pulled the truck up too much, the truck would be in danger of sliding into the river. If we let it down too far, we risked crushing the rescuers.

The flight engineer became our eyes. "Okay, sir, I dropped the sling. You are drifting right. Hold, hold. ...Okay, they've got the sling connected to the truck. Bring her up slowly... Truck is coming up. Hold. Okay, very slowly, come up a little more. Hold. ...Okay, rescuers are under the cab. Hold. Hold."

The next few minutes seemed like an eternity. We simply couldn't afford to move laterally, or up or down. My muscles were sore from the tension, but there's no way I could relax. Finally, after being on site about fifteen minutes, we heard: "Sir, the G.I.s are free of the truck." A moment later we got confirmation over the radio, and we were able to let the truck down again. I had hardly dared to breathe while our delicate mission was in progress, but a huge wave of relief washed over me when it was over. One of the guys had been killed instantly when the accident occurred—the truck had crushed him. The other was rushed to a hospital. We later heard he was going to be okay. I felt bad the one G.I. hadn't made it, but at the same time was so grateful that we could have a key role in the survival of the other one. We also found out it had taken just nine minutes after we got the call until we were hovering over the truck by the Hue bridge.*

Later that afternoon found us back at the Locker Room. As I relaxed in my hootch, I thought, *What a day for my first official mission as an AC.* My aircraft and crew

*I am indebted to Tom Hirschler for his recollections of this mission which can be found at www.geronimos.org/varsity/VarsityStories .

had been instrumental in saving a person's life. It was a very good, efficient job by the whole crew, working as a team. A "well done!" was passed down to us from our division and battalion commanders. This was probably my most satisfying day since coming to Vietnam.

Many years later, the flight engineer on this mission, Darryl Murray, shared his recollections of the day: "I remember the urgency of the mission and how quickly we reacted as a team...

"It was a ballet and symphony of form and function. [Hirschler's] and Petersen's reactions to my commands were perfection of motion... [J]ust one slight move the wrong way would have killed the survivor whose legs were pinned under the edge of the bed of the truck. A lift too high or too far forward would have spun the truck on top of him. I flew with a lot of pilots... All were great on the controls, but that morning, [Petersen and Hirschler] were the best.

"You know how loud the inside of a Chinook is and how the sound-deadening effect of wearing the flight helmet virtually blocks out all outside noise. Well, I will never forget the scream of that soldier as we gingerly lifted the truck up and the blood flow returned to his legs. I would have never thought that someone could make a noise as loud as a Chinook one hundred or so feet above him, but it happened and I still hear him to this day. I'm just glad we had the opportunity to make that happen for him. I wish we could have done the same for the one that didn't make it."**

**E-mail from Darryl Murray, 09 November 2004.

Chapter 21

...even the darkness will not be dark to
you;
the night will shine like the day...

--Psalm 139:12 (NIV)

24 January 1970

As of this day I was "over the hump." Well, maybe it wasn't until the twenty-fifth. I had left the States on July 25 last year, but my DEROS would be July 24 of this year. I audaciously decided to claim it for today — half of my tour was now behind me.

I was on stand-by this evening for flare missions. That was a rather new mission for us. We had had a short training session (orientation was more like it) several days ago. The training was mainly for the flight engineers on how to handle the large flares, how to set them to begin illumination, etc. The primary focus for flare missions was to provide night-time illumination for units in the bush who needed it due to their tactical situation. Our Chinooks were to be used as first responders until Air Force C-130s could get to the party and take over for us. We could be on station in our AO quite a bit sooner than the C-130s, but the C-130s could carry more flares and loiter longer than we could. That's not to say there wouldn't be times that we would fly the whole mission; this did happen from time to time. But it was more effective to have Chinooks and C-130s work in conjunction.

But tonight came at the end of a crazy past week. Late the previous Monday night (January 19), right after I had gone to sleep, we had all been awakened for an immediate stand-by. Apparently higher headquarters had received intelligence that a large ground assault was about to take place near Dong Ha up on the "Z," and we would be needed to lift reinforcements in there in the middle of the night. But in the end, no attack had actually taken place, and we'd never taken off.

Ever since then, and until February 15, every available aircraft with crew would be on a thirty-minute stand-by, twenty-four hours a day. This was because of intelligence concerns with the up-and-coming Tet season and an anticipated increase of enemy activity. So we wouldn't be the only ones on stand-by that evening.

Right around 2100, I heard the ops officer call out, "We gotta launch the flare bird! Hey, Petersen, get your crew and get airborne." I got the map coordinates for the mission, a thumbnail sketch of the situation, and the radio frequency for our ground contact.

When I got to the aircraft, the crew was already there. I quickly pinpointed our destination on the map, southeast of the Ashau Valley—nothing but mountains and jungle out there. I told the crew what I knew about our mission: a patrol had run into some heavy contact and had requested illumination. They needed to be extracted by some slicks—UH-1 Hueys—if possible.

We cranked up as quickly as possible and were airborne in no time. We got a vector from ground radar and climbed up through the clouds to seven thousand feet, which was above the cloud layer. The moon was shining brightly; it was one of the most beautiful sights I'd ever seen. I made contact with the grunts; the radio operator sounded surprisingly calm. I told him we'd be there in about five minutes and would start dropping flares right away.

We were notified by air traffic control when we were over the drop zone. "Okay, start dropping flares," I said. We set up our orbit, and ground radar kept us over the drop zone.

"Hey, Varsity, you need to set your flares to start burning a bit lower. They're burning out by the time they get out of the clouds," crackled the radio from our ground contact.

"Roger, we'll correct that." I depressed the radio switch for intercom and said, "Hey chief, the flares are burning too high. They're burning out before they're out of the clouds."

"Okay, sir, we'll adjust them."

After a couple minutes, I contacted the guys on the ground again. "Are you getting some illumination now?"

"Yeah, we got a lot of light down here now. One flare was still burning when it hit the ground, but I think that's as good as you can get it."

"Roger." Again I relayed onto the intercom: "Hey chief, we about got it, but they had one still burning when it hit the ground. Can you adjust it up just a little?"

"Will do, sir."

We continued on our racetrack pattern, dropping flares at regular intervals. The beauty of the night sky as we saw it belied what was happening below. A few minutes later we got another call from the ground. A whispering voice said, "The bad guys are really close to us. I think we're gonna try to bust out of here."

"Roger, understand. Do you need us to do anything else for you, contact anyone?"

"No, just keep dropping those flares."

Within a few more minutes, we were contacted by a C-130 which was going to relieve us. We provided him a short sitrep, and he made contact with the grunts. We returned to the Locker Room where our aircraft was reloaded with flares should we get called out on another mission. I headed for my hootch and bed. We later heard that the patrol we'd supported on our mission had been extracted but didn't hear if they had any casualties.

Chapter 22

Life will be brighter than noonday,
and darkness will become like morning.

--Job 11:17 (NIV)

28 Jan. 70

Dear Donna,

It's a warm, sunny morning…. The past four or five days we've had clear, blue skies and pleasant temperatures: around 80. I just love it, but I'm afraid it won't last long. I'm almost ashamed of myself for telling you this since you've been experiencing such icy cold weather. I just love flying when I can…climb and climb into the endless beauty of the blue skies. Maybe this is signaling the end of the monsoon season, but I have my doubts. Well, here's hoping.

…[Yesterday] I had an extended lunch hour because of mission times. A bunch of us guys ate a quick lunch and then went sunbathing! We all got on our swimsuits or cutoffs, got our radios, and went on top of the bunker for about 1½ hours. There's quite a bit of sand on top of the bunker (from broken sandbags), so it seemed just like we were at the beach (well, almost like it). I got a partial sunburn on my lily-white bodd. Oh, well, if I can lay in the sun with some regularity for six months, I should be able to come home with a good ol' suntan.

We're still on our alert as we will be until the middle of Feb. There hasn't been much of any activity yet, although almost everyone is anticipating some. There have been reports of large concentrations of gooks in the Ashau Valley. [There have] been a lot of air strikes by B-52s and Air Force fighters along with helicopter gunships in the Ashau.

…I am not pulling your leg. I did go to see a car dealer in Da Nang. Maybe I should have said car representative…most of the automotive corporations have representatives at many of the PXs in Nam. They take orders for new cars while you are here. Then you'll have a new car

waiting when you get home. You can get real good discounts ordering this way. I'm thinking pretty strongly on a GTO.

...I won't be flying for a couple days now since payday is coming up, and I'm the payroll officer...

Love, Dale

*   *   *

1 Feb. 70

Dear Donna,

...My head is still spinning, as busy as I've been. I've been payroll officer, but they've also had me flying. We've got so much to do, and right now we have a shortage of pilots. I flew two nights in a row on flare missions. I get awfully tired, but I really shouldn't complain. We've also had a couple red alerts in the middle of the night which serves to cut down on sleep. I'll be glad to get things back to normal, although the time has really flown by these past few busy days.

It's morning now, and the only reason I'm not flying is because my ship had maintenance problems. I did get some time in earlier this morning but I had a beep failure...the beep controls your engine and, more specifically, your rotor RPM, and you've just got to have that. So, I figured that I'd take advantage of this break and get a few lines written to you...

Love, Dale

*   *   *

5 Feb. 70

Dear Donna,

...[M]y R & R allocation just came down. I'll be going to Sydney [Australia] from March 17 to 24. I think I'll be ready for it by then. Also, when I get back, I'll only have four months left to go over here.

I remember you asking me about our unit patch a little while ago, and then I forgot to include it in my letter. Well, you're right: the 101st Division's patch does have an eagle on it. That's why we're known as Screaming Eagles...We have another name for it, but I can't say it in the presence of ladies...

We've got our good weather yet. Before yesterday, I flew two days with "the old man" (our company commander). Even though he is the C.O., I'm an aircraft commander, and he's only a pilot (he doesn't fly very often). Therefore I was in command while we were flying...

I...got your happy letter about exams being over...I can't believe where kids are going on semester breaks nowadays. Whenever I had a semester break, I'd...grab my shotgun and go hunting, go ice-skating or work. I guess that's what becomes of the affluent society (Don't I sound like a conservative old fogey...)

Love, Pete

Chapter 23

This is the day which the Lord hath made;
We will rejoice and be glad in it.

--Psalm 118:24 (KJV)

mid-February 1970

The day was just dawning. There was enough light to see my way up the small hill toward the revetment where today's assigned aircraft had spent the night. The stars were winking out, but it would be several minutes before the sun came up. The small mountain to the east which separated Camp Eagle from Phu Bai was silhouetted against a yellowish-red glow in the sky. I paused a moment to take in the simple beauty of this new day. My soul felt good, maybe even revived. I smiled to no one in particular; perhaps it was to God. When I got to my helicopter, I pulled out my camera and captured it on film.

I couldn't wait to be airborne, but we first needed to pull our pre-flight inspection. Soon we were in the cockpit and the turbine engines were starting to whine. The rotor blades flexed, then started a slow rotation. The rotation speed increased rapidly, then they were at flight RPM. A couple minutes later I said into my helmet mike: "Clear me for a vertical takeoff."

The door gunners and flight engineer all chimed in with their clearances. I nudged the thrust lever upward and the front wheels came off the ground. A little more nudging and the helicopter was airborne. I kept pulling upward and the Chinook leaped vertically, as if it had limitless power and nothing could hold it down. After I was about one hundred feet over the now empty revetment, I pushed forward on the cyclic, and we headed out beyond the Camp Eagle perimeter as we continued our climb. Just then the sun was beginning its morning ascent out of the South China Sea into the blue heavens of Southeast Asia. We were now speeding at 150 knots toward the Hue Citadel and beyond to the DMZ. A morning like this made me happy to be an aviator, happy to be alive.

We arrived at Quang Tri and it was time to go to work. There were several sorties of the typical ammo, food and water re-supply to be flown to firebases in this sector. One early sortie brought us close to Laos. There was a small outpost west of Khe Sanh that needed some supplies. It was a real no-man's land, nothing but jagged peaks, deep valleys, and jungle. I was glad to have a couple Cobra helicopter gunships along as an escort. A couple hours and several sorties later, we were assigned to carry some ARVN troops into various locations where they were conducting sweeps. There were several Chinooks working this mission since we had upwards of a couple battalions to move. The ARVNs had been running into quite a bit of contact, and they'd been keeping Charlie on the run, or so we'd been told. Perhaps Vietnamization, the U.S. policy to turn over more combat responsibility to the ARVNs, was working.

We set down on a sandy strip in an ARVN base camp and were waiting for our next load. About that time, an ARVN Huey landed about fifty yards in front of us where crew members unceremoniously dumped an ARVN soldier, then took off again. I couldn't take my eyes off him as he lay there on his back. A dark circle, a little larger than a softball, had spread out from the center of his chest, staining his fatigue top. He was only a single body among hundreds of thousands of casualties, but I couldn't help wondering how long it would take a loved one to find out that he was a KIA. Was his mother nearby? Was she even alive? Was there a girlfriend, or even a wife? Did he have a son or a daughter? Did they miss him and were they even now wondering when he'd be coming home on leave? If they had any hope, were they thinking of the day this would all be over and he could help in the rice paddies again? Did they have dreams of his getting an education and a good job?

Freddie Latremore, my pilot, must have been having some of the same thoughts. He turned his radio switch to transmit, and said to the Aussie advisor who was our contact, "Sorry about your little buddy there."

"Thanks for that, Mate. He got it last night. The war's over for him now."

It was time for our departure, and I had no alternative but to pull up to a hover. As I did, the tremendous winds off our rotor blades blew sand over the body.

By mid-afternoon we were working out of Camp Evans, which was south of where we'd been working earlier in the day—roughly halfway between Quang Tri and Camp Eagle. AFVN had just finished their "cowboy hour"—nothing but country and western music. As far as I was concerned, they could finish with the cowboy tunes permanently. AFVN seemed to be forever having some contest for a Buck Owens jacket during that hour; I couldn't figure out who'd want one. I guess there were plenty of older guys in Nam who liked the country and western music much more than the hard rock which was on most of the time, but not me. Besides, I needed to pay attention to all the radio traffic, not to music.

It wasn't too much later that our UHF radio crackled to life again: "This is Hotel on Guard. Arc Light, Arc Light, commencing in zero five minutes. Max ord, fifty thousand feet." Freddie jotted down the coordinates.

"A B-52 strike. Where's it at, Freddie?"

After a few seconds of checking the map coordinates, he said, "Looks to be about ten miles west of our location. We should be okay."

I had heard guys talk about seeing a B-52 bombing run in progress, of witnessing the destructive power of several B-52s flying in formation and dropping their huge bomb loads at the same time. As I flew I could see the side of a mountain torn to shreds by what had to have been such a strike. I imagined what it would be like to witness a B-52 strike: the whole side of a mountain erupting. A line of explosions progressing from left to right, like soldiers marching in ranks, kicking up dust as they went. The deep green of the triple canopy jungle on the mountainside turning into a wildly chaotic jumble of browns and grays and greens. Watching in fascinated horror at the power and utter desolation unleashed in just a few moments of time.

By late afternoon we were back at the Locker Room. Another day in I Corps had come and gone, and new images had been burned into my brain.

Chapter 24

*[The Lord] maketh me to lie down in
green pastures:
He leadeth me beside the still waters
…though I walk through the valley of
the shadow of death…*

--Psalm 23:2, 4a (KJV)

20 Feb. 70

Dear Donna,

Here I am, sitting on a firebase with nothing to do, so thought this would be a good time to write you a letter. Now, I know you have all kinds of questions in your mind, so I'll try to answer them. My mission today is known as a ready reaction force. They do this every time a dignitary is in the area. They have a platoon of infantry ready to go (on my Chinook) in case the dignitary's bird should go down. Should this happen (I know it <u>won't</u> happen) I would lift the platoon into the area to provide security. They also have a bunch of gunships and a medivac ship on standby alert for the same thing. It's a bunch of baloney if you ask me. The dignitary today is Gen. Abrams (Commander in Chief in Vietnam). I guess he'll be flying around this area for awhile.

I'm in quite a beautiful setting at the moment. We're out at a firebase which is on top of a high hill in the lowlands...[B]elow us a beautiful river is winding its way down a lush valley covered with trees. In the background, the mountains are rising majestically. The birds are singing. It seems so hard to fathom that this beautiful, bucolic setting is really so unfriendly. It's a real shame. Oops! I just got a rude awakening from my lulling, dreamy little world. The artillery on top of the hill are blasting away on another fire mission. The birds are no longer singing. I can see the artillery rounds impacting far off on the side of a mountain...[T]he river and mountains seem foreboding instead of friendly and inviting. The firing has now stopped, at least for the time being. There was probably a living, breathing body a few seconds ago. Now I imagine there is just a twisted, broken form...The sun is now shining brightly. The sky is a beautiful blue. This is a land of many contrasts.

> *Must go now... Take care...*
> *Love, Dale*

Chapter 25

…Give me relief from my distress…

--Psalm 4:1 (NIV)

3 Mar. 70

Dear Donna,

I'm afraid this is gonna have to be a shortie again. It's not real late, but I'm just beat. I just gotta get something written to you, though. It's been a few days again. I started writing you last night but fell asleep at the desk. I'm sorry. I gotta keep telling myself that maybe you worry when you don't hear from me for a few days, so I'll let you know that I'm just fine, other than being a little weary.

I think there may be something wrong with me 'cause I just don't eat anymore, no appetite. 'Course with the food we get, that's not too hard to imagine…You know, I get so tired sometimes that I'll wake up in the middle of the night and won't get back to sleep for a long time. I just toss and turn and feel rotten. Then I'm tired all day. When I'm tired, I get tense, and my nerves are on edge. I just don't understand. I'll be skinny as a scarecrow. Boy, now I'm sounding like an old lady who talks herself into chronic illness. Enough of that.

Our mail service is getting screwed up again. Hardly any mail has come in for almost a week. I haven't heard from you for that long a time, and I know how often you write.

I guess I spoke too soon about the weather. The monsoon season hasn't ended yet. We've got rain, drizzle, fog, low clouds, poor visibility: you name it, we've got it. It's little things like this that get me down. I just gotta get out of this place for awhile. I'd swear that every helicopter in the division was trying to hit me yesterday and today. With the poor visibility, you can't see another aircraft until he's almost right on top of you. Other aircraft are more dangerous than Charlie.

I just gotta get to bed. This wasn't a very pleasant letter. Please believe me that I'm not always a big complainer. Remember that I am always thinking of you. Wish so much that I could be there, enjoy your companionship, see your beautiful self, feel your warmth and softness. Won't be long now...

Love, Dale

*　　　*　　　*

6 Mar. 70

Dear Donna,

I'm convinced that the mail service is screwed up now. Yesterday I got five, count 'em — 1, 2, 3, 4, 5 letters from you. They were dated from Feb. 19-Feb. 25. Somebody in the U.S. post office hangs onto my mail for a couple days, then sends them on...Anyway, it's really great compensation to get five letters in one day. I'm so flabbergasted, I don't know where to begin.

...So, you went through all your summer clothes, and you don't need a thing, huh? Well, I went through mine, and I'm the same way as you — plenty of fatigues to last me. Course, there's a new lightweight jungle fatigue on the market now which I saw at the fashion show the other day. I may just buy some. (???)

I can't believe that you've never had a Coney Island before. I've been eating them since I was knee-high to a grasshopper. They're good, but there's nothing like a good ol' Shakey's pizza with appropriate beverage...

I gotta knock off for now. It's flying time again. Take care now.

Love, Dale

179

*　　　*　　　*

13 Mar. 70

Dear Donna,

I know you're about ready to give up on me, if you haven't already. Whatever you may think of my poor writing ways, remember one thing: I am thinking of you almost constantly. It seems like it's harder and harder to get my letters written. We continue to be busy, but of course we're not busy all the time. Sometimes I don't do anything but talk with my roomie, trying to relax, and then flopping in[to] bed. I usually try to watch the movie whenever I can since it usually helps me unwind...

I've got lots of letters from you again since I last wrote, as usual. There's nothing I enjoy more than when the mail comes in and I have something from you. I don't think you'll ever realize how much more livable this tour has been for me because of all the many, many beautiful letters you have written to me. For this I will never be able to thank you enough.

Well, in another few short days I'll be living like a civilian again [because of my R & R to Australia]. Ah, what bliss. And, yes, I will get 8 hours of sleep and eat 3 meals a day. In fact, I'll probably sleep more than that, and I definitely will eat more than three times a day. I think I'll eat filet mignon most of the time, interspersed with other types of steaks. Then I'll eat some pizzas and lots of other good things. Oh, yes, room service will bring me my breakfast every morning. I'll stay at about the most expensive hotel I can find. I'll spend a lot of time at the beach, and also at the zoo watching the kangaroos and koala bears...

Thanks for the St. Pat's Day card. Also the love beads. You know, I really appreciate them, especially since I know how they were given. But, I won't be able to wear them. The Army thinks they mean you're an anti-war hippie if you wear them...

Love, Dale

Chapter 26

…the mountain was ablaze with fire…

--Deuteronomy 5:23 (NIV)

15 March 1970

It was another hot day. In some ways I missed those days in the heart of the monsoon season when we had to wear jackets and my little electric heater was on full blast. But I sure appreciated the clear skies on a day like today. Plus, the sweat factor was only high until the rotor blades started turning. Then we could get some pleasant breezes through our cockpit windows. One old flight instructor told me once that the rotating rotor head of a helicopter was just like a big fan when you were in flight: "If you don't believe that, just think how much you'll be sweating if that rotor head stops turning." That joke must have had a thousand fathers.

Today was a great day because it would be my last day of flying before my R & R. Tomorrow I would catch the bus run to Da Nang and from there would be flying to Sydney, Australia for a week! I couldn't wait!

I had a unique mission this day, something I'd not done before. As briefed previously, I'd be doing foo gas drops on bad-guy bunker complexes. Foo gas was similar to napalm—jellied gasoline—only foo gas was less jellied. The idea was to burn the complex so that it couldn't be used again. The complex was supposed to be unoccupied, but because of it's location in Indian country (Charlie's territory) near the Ashau Valley, I'd also have gunship escorts.

We landed at our staging area before picking up our first load, because we were going to have a chemical officer with us for this mission. For each sortie, we'd pick up a sling load of foo gas in fifty-gallon drums. Once the donut of the net was attached to the cargo hook on the helicopter, the flight engineer would attach another part of the net to the helicopter, but away from the hook. Then when we were over the target area, we'd activate the cargo hook to release the load, in this case opening the net rather than dropping it completely, since it was still partly attached to the helicopter. This would allow the foo gas drums to tumble to the ground with much greater dispersion than if we'd simply dropped the load intact, drums and net.

"I'll be in the jump seat up front with you," the chem guy said to me. "I'll identify your target drop area. Also, since I've done this type of mission before, I'll help you with sighting your release so we can hit the target. When you're on your drop run, you'll need to be a couple hundred feet AGL and about eighty knots indicated airspeed. Rather primitive, but it works."

Then he turned to the flight engineer: "You'll need to be over the cargo hole when we're on our drop run. You'll need to have a smoke grenade in your hand which will be the igniter for the foo gas. The aircraft commander will activate the hook for the drop. As soon as you see the hook open up, drop your smoke grenade. If all goes according to plan, the smoke grenade will hit the ground just as the drums are busting open and dispersing the foo gas."

We needed to get going soon for our predetermined rendezvous time with our Cobra gunship escorts. We picked up our load and headed toward the Ashau. Our flight was over familiar, rugged territory, incredibly majestic except for the scars from artillery and bombs. As we neared our objective, we made contact with our escorts. There were four helicopter gunships that met us, plus two Air Force F-4 Phantoms circling high overhead.

As we neared the target area, the chem officer pointed out the first bunker area for our drop. I couldn't see any bunkers per se, but he described a couple natural features we'd use as an aiming point. I circled around and started a descent to our drop altitude. As I leveled out for our drop run, two Cobras moved into position on either side of me.

"Okay, chief, we're on our target run," I said over the intercom.

"Roger, ready with the smoke."

"Do you see the target?" our passenger asked.

"I've got it," I said.

I maintained eighty knots. The chem guy leaned forward. "Okay, you're almost there. Get ready. Release."

I punched the hook release button on my cyclic stick grip. "Drums and smoke are away," said the flight engineer. A couple seconds later, confirmation came: "The foo gas ignited."

I yanked up on the thrust control lever and the Chinook rapidly gained altitude. I initiated a left turn so I could see the drop area. Thick black smoke was billowing from a broad area in the impact zone. Within the heart of the smoke, an incandescent orange glow indicated the searing intensity of the fire. It jogged my memory back to the time I was introduced to Dante's *Inferno* in a high school English class.

"Good dispersion," the chem guy said. "Chinooks really work well for a mission like this. We can drop a lot of drums of foo gas per sortie."

We flew a couple more sorties. On the last sortie for the mission the foo gas failed to ignite. "Toro, this is Varsity, do you suppose you could fire up that last drop we did?"

"Roger, we're already rolling in on it."

I watched as the Cobra approached the drop zone. Then he cut loose with a burst from his mini-gun, a gatling-type gun which could fire six thousand rounds per minute. Thanks to the fact that tracer rounds were embedded with the other rounds, the foo gas quickly ignited. We circled the area a couple times so the chemical officer could get a good look at the target area and make his assessment. "Looks like we got some good coverage. That should do it for today."

After dropping him off at the staging area, we headed for the Camp Eagle refueling pads, topped off our tanks, and brought her home to the Locker Room. And I breathed a sigh of relief. "Australia, here I come!"

Chapter 27

He leadeth me beside the still waters;
He restoreth my soul…

--Psalm 23:2b-3a (KJV)

16-23 March 1970

My journey to Australia almost got off to a very bad start—apparently the monsoons still weren't over, because on the morning of March 16, I woke up to darkness, drizzle, and just plain old nasty weather. It was so bad I was afraid the bus run wouldn't fly and I wouldn't make it to Da Nang that day. But the weather did lift a bit, the bus run did fly, and, best of all, I was on it.

I spent that night at the R & R Processing Center in Da Nang, and most of the next day. While there was the inevitable Army paper work to fill out, most of the time I was just hanging around waiting for my flight to Sydney. I was so excited to be getting away from Vietnam for a few days. It was a bit like a little kid waiting for his first plane ride.

My eight-hour flight on a World Airways chartered DC-8 to Australia left that evening, March 17. Everyone was in a good mood, which was no surprise. We were served a steak dinner which I expected would be only the first of many in the next week. After I had settled down I managed to get a little sleep, then saw one of the most beautiful sunrises I'd seen in a long time, about an hour before we arrived in Sydney. We had a bit of a rude awakening when we got to customs. We were required to open all our baggage for in-depth inspections. Then a number of guys were selected for full strip searches in small rooms. I suppose this was a result of G.I.s previously trying to smuggle drugs or pot into the country. After we cleared customs, we were ushered into an auditorium where we got a briefing on how we were to conduct ourselves, what kinds of activities were available in the area, transportation options, and a myriad of other information. We were provided extensive details about lodging options, almost all of which were in the Kings Cross area of Sydney, which catered to a younger crowd and had a lot of night life. My home for six nights would be the Top of the Cross Travelodge. We were also given the opportunity to rent some civilian clothing which most of us did since few of us had very much of our own in Vietnam.

I spent the better part of my first day in Sydney getting settled in my room—which was even nicer and more comfortable than I had imagined—and looking around the King's Cross area. It was very crowded but had a clean, respectable feel to it. I didn't know whether or not to be surprised that I didn't see any hippies around. That evening I had dinner with a Marine I had met on the bus to the hotel. We both tied into huge steaks and relished every minute of it. Afterward we just mingled with the crowds and went to a couple different discotheques and enjoyed the atmosphere of people and rock music. More than once we were asked: "Are you Yanks?" Our haircuts were a dead giveaway. The people were friendly and relaxed, almost like one big happy family. Any tension I still had in my body seemed to drain away.

The next morning, and the rest of my mornings in Sydney, I slept in late—usually until 10 or 11 a.m. Then I would have breakfast brought up to my room. Did that ever seem like a luxury! And since I didn't have my mother or my commanding officer telling me to go to bed, I often stayed out late, until I started falling asleep on my feet, which actually wasn't very late my first few days in Australia.

While I did take some time to explore different areas of Sydney, every day found me at the beach. Sydney was a few miles inland from the ocean beaches. I would take a cab to the city quay on Sydney harbor and take either a fast ride on a hydroplane or a slower-paced cruise on a ferry. I enjoyed stopping on a couple of occasions at a pleasant old pub near the beach for a sandwich and a beer.

The month of March was the end of summer for Sydney. Even though the temperatures were an enjoyable 75° to 80° during my stay, the beaches were not at all crowded. Toward the end of the afternoon they would be virtually deserted. I had mixed feelings of loneliness and gratitude that I could be by myself for awhile. It gave me time to think, to enjoy life in the dream world I was formulating in my mind. The waves would roar as they crashed on sandbars, yet the water would barely murmur when it finally reached the shore, then it would subside. The water and sand sort of mingled together around my feet as I walked along the shore line. It was so pleasurable to not be wearing a hat so I could feel the wind blowing in my hair (which was starting to get long by Army standards). I did not want to leave this paradise—it was probably one of my happiest moments in over eight months.

The only frightening thing about Sydney was the traffic. In Australia, they drive on the "wrong" side of the road. More than once I had close calls because I would look the wrong way before crossing the street. And then there were the cab rides—Sydney cab drivers had a well-earned reputation for being crazy drivers. I would find myself in the back seat of a cab, hurtling down the middle of a narrow city street, watching an approaching car, and leaning to the right as if to help the driver get over so that the two vehicles could safely pass. Instead, I would panic (momentarily) as the driver moved left. Somehow I survived all that, and in six quick days it was over.

When it was finally March 23, I could hardly believe it was my last day already. I was really going to hate going back, but my flight from Sydney to Da Nang was leaving at 0700 tomorrow. I was almost surprised at what an enjoyable time I'd had on my R & R. I think the main reason it had been so pleasant was that I'd been able to relax in civilization for a few days and forget about my other life for awhile. I believe it helped that Australia was much more like home than if I'd chosen a more exotic destination like Thailand or Hong Kong for my R & R. I had one overriding, very exciting thought, though—there were a mere four months left before I would get on my Freedom Bird back to the world.

*   *   *

28 Mar. 70

Dear Donna,

Here it is Saturday..., and I've been back into the swing of things for three days already. We left Sydney Tuesday morning and got into Da Nang late that evening. I got back to my company late the following day. They put me back to work right away. Early the next morning I was strapped into my familiar cockpit again, flying to and fro from Hue to the DMZ and from the coast throughout the mountains. I know you aren't gonna believe this, but it felt good to be flying again. I know, I know: I'm crazy. But I just love flying. (I'd rather do my flying in the States, though.)

Well, I've been flying steady for three days now. I don't feel nearly as exhausted as I did before I went to Sydney, so I guess that is what I needed. Everything looks just a little brighter now, so I know R & R helped. The best thing is that I now have <u>less</u> than four months to go. I can hardly believe that I've been here over eight months already. If I keep flying lots, and if I can keep somewhat of a bright outlook on things, the time should really continue to sail.

Even the weather hasn't dampened my spirits much. You know, the weather was perfectly clear all over Vietnam until I got <u>north</u> of Da Nang, into our ol' stomping grounds. Sure enough, all of a sudden there were dark, low clouds, rain, and everything nice. I could not believe it. The old monsoons are still hanging on...

Love, Dale

Chapter 28

*Question: What is your only comfort in
life and in death?*

*Answer: That I am not my own, but
belong—body and soul,
in life and in death—to my faithful
Savior Jesus Christ…*

--Q and A 1, Heidelberg Catechism

Dale H. Petersen

8 Apr. 70

Dear Donna,

I was gonna write you a real neat, pleasant letter, but I can find no pleasant words this evening. Please forgive me. I don't know where to start or what to say. I probably won't even send this letter, so it really doesn't matter. If anyone tells you that there is no war anymore, just smack 'em in the mouth. The brass are really proud of this week's casualty list: <u>only</u> 106 died in action. I'm sure that the widows and mothers of those 106 who died this week will be happy to hear that their deceased son, husband, or father was one of only 106 killed this week. The stupidity, the senselessness of this destruction of life is appalling. Maybe if it were a truth under the pretext of helping the Vietnamese people, it wouldn't seem so bad. But when it seems to turn out to be an attempt by some brass who is trying to build up his career, and in the process lives are sacrificed, it's downright nauseating. I'm sorry. Enough of that.

I don't know what kind of war news you get or how comprehensive it is, but I thought I'd tell you just a little so you will not worry when you read about it because I'm just fine. You may read about a heavy increase of action in northern I Corps, not only along the DMZ, but also further south. You may read about some firebases being overrun. No firebases here were actually completely overrun, but there has been some fierce fighting. Allied casualties have increased, but nothing like the NVA or VC "box score." There have been a few helicopters shot down, including a couple Chinooks. The only reason I tell you this is to tell you I wasn't involved in case you should read about it. I'm just fine, really...

Love, Dale

*　　*　　*

9 April 1970

I couldn't believe that I had actually sent that letter I wrote to Donna last night. I could be such an idiot sometimes. I sounded like such a whiner. I knew I had to start using some better judgment. I felt worried what to write Mom and Dad. Dad always followed the news and knew what was going on. And if he knew something about increased action in Vietnam, especially in I Corps, he'd tell Mom about it. I decided to just keep writing "happy face" letters and say all is well with me. Because it was. I wasn't going to start writing war news stuff now. Mom worried enough the way it was. I could tell them more stuff when I got home, if I needed to.

"Hey, Petey person, let's go get some chow," Phil said.

I swung my legs over the side of my bunk and sat up. I grabbed my hat, shoved it down on my head, and walked out the door.

After we went through the line, we sat down at a table in the officers' side of the mess hall. "Hey, did you guys hear about Evans?" someone was saying.

"The flight engineer?"

"Yeah. He got wounded."

"What?" My brain was having a hard time reckoning with this foreign message.

"They were in an LZ and took some hits."

I glanced at my food tray and felt a wave of nausea. "How is he?"

"I think okay. I think they got him to a MASH unit at Camp Evans."

I wanted to sense that everything would be okay, but I couldn't get my mind off the wound. "Who was flying?"

"Dave Magers was the AC."

"Is he married?" That seemed like a dumb question the minute I asked it, but for some unknown reason I felt the need to keep talking about it.

"Yeah, I think so. Think his wife had a kid he hasn't seen yet."

Evans had flown with me several times. He was a pretty quiet kid, about my age. A good troop who did his job. He'd been around for several months. I could picture him going about his duties, climbing on top of the fuselage to do a preflight check, sharing a joke with the crew chiefs, talking me down over a load of ammo to get it hooked up. I just couldn't square those images with one of him lying in a hospital bed.

A little later that evening we had our usual pilots' meeting in our O club. A very sober looking Dave Magers was relating what had happened.

"We were at a hover and took some small arms fire. One round hit Evans in the side—just missed his chicken plate, just behind it. He seemed to be doing okay. We got him to the MASH at Camp Evans in just a few minutes." I could picture Camp Evans in my mind, having flown resupply missions out of there many times. We would often refuel there or shut down for a quick break to eat some C-rations… But I tried to keep my focus on Dave as he continued his tale, just in time to hear, "He walked off the aircraft on his own. He died about an hour later."

What? Wait a minute! They said Evans was okay. He walked off the aircraft by himself! How can this be? It can't be! How can a guy walk off a helicopter and be dead an hour later? No answer to my question, no relief for my mind or heart. *Oh, Lord, what's going on? Make it not be! Why did it just miss his chicken plate? That's why we wear those things: to stop a round!*

In contrast to the jumble of thoughts raging in my mind, I didn't say a thing. No one was saying much. I had been in country, in Varsity, for over eight months, and in that time our company never even had a guy wounded. And now we had a KIA. This was totally new for most of us. I felt a shiver throughout my entire body. Tightness in my muscles, tightness in my gut…thought I might puke. Breathing felt like work. *Get a hold of yourself. Everyone looks kinda downcast but not like they are losing it. Knock it off, Petersen, just breathe normal, be normal. Don't be an idiot.*

I was eventually successful in stuffing my feelings and put on a stoic mask.

The next day the company had a short memorial service. We lined up in ranks in front of the maintenance hangar. In front of us was just a small, ordinary, Army-issue table. Major Cone, our CO, walked up to the table carrying a flight helmet. He set the helmet on the table. "David Paul Evans, born Dec. 28, 1947…"

I didn't hear much of what he or the chaplain said. I kept seeing a re-run in my mind, of a round just missing a chicken plate by an inch or so, of a kid walking off a Chinook on his own. And I wondered about a new young widow, and a little baby who would never see its Dad. I didn't even know if it was a boy or girl ...

Chapter 29

...the Spirit helps us in our weakness;
for we do not know how to pray as we
ought,
but the Spirit himself intercedes for
us
with sighs too deep for words.

--Romans 8:26 (RSV)

11 April 1970

It had been another long day of flying. Most of my missions had been around the Ashau Valley. Both the Ashau and the DMZ area were hot with combat. I was thankful that I wasn't a grunt or a cannon cocker. The artillery guys on those lonely firebases on ridgelines or mountaintops always seemed quite vulnerable to me when I brought in sling loads. Chuck would often try to penetrate their wire at night or just light 'em up with small arms and mortars. Firebase Fuller, which sat atop a mountaintop virtually on the DMZ, was taking mortars and other fire daily. We weren't even supposed to go in there without a gunship escort. Fuller was the worst of the worst for the time being.

Our guys were sure putting out a lot of HE (high explosives) from their 105mm and 155mm artillery guns. That's a main reason why we'd been having so many more missions over the past few weeks. It didn't help that the 101st had begun establishing a lot more firebases with the advent of the dry season (at least I hoped the monsoons were over). We brought them most of their supplies, but I guessed the vast majority of our loads lately had been artillery rounds. Oh, yes, my prediction (and everyone else's) had come true—after giving up most of the mountain terrain to the bad guys the previous fall at the approach of the monsoons, we were now well on our way to taking back that same territory again.

I had flown this day with one of the new guys. It was a fact of life that new guys cycled in as the old hands went back to the world at tour's end. I was one of the more experienced ACs, an old hand at twenty-one years old, so I tended to get some of the newer guys. I tried to think of how it was when I'd been a newbie in August and September of 1969. I tried to be patient but wasn't always as successful as I wanted to be. It was my goal to give them as much stick time as possible, but mostly I wanted to pass on what I'd learned about staying alive and keeping the aircraft safe. Having said that, I had to admit that I was guilty of "cowboying" the aircraft lately. For example, I'd sometimes approach a refueling pad at a low level with a high rate of airspeed. Then I'd do a big flare and bottom out my thrust lever, and try to stop the aircraft at a hover right over the pad. Not that I considered it all that unsafe, but it wouldn't have been tolerated in the States.

Richard Van De Warker was a pilot who had been in country about three weeks. I was glad to see that he already had decent control of the aircraft and could fly a sling load sortie okay. Around mid-afternoon I took a turn and went to pick up a load at the supply staging area. I brought the Chinook over the load, was hooked up, and took the slack out of the sling. As I started to lift the load, I noticed that the rotor RPM was starting to bleed off. I squeezed the intercom transmit button on my cyclic stick and said, "Watch my beep, watch my beep!" The RPM was still bleeding off, putting the aircraft in danger of crashing if the situation wasn't remedied. I glanced down at the radio control panel and noticed that

Richard's intercom receiver switch was turned off. I glanced at him and saw he had a big smile on his face and was talking on his radio. I reached across and whacked him on his shoulder. He had a startled, shocked look on his face as I pointed angrily at his rotor tachometer. He jumped noticeably, then got on the beep switch and quickly brought the rotor RPM back to a safe operating range. I was hot under the collar, probably more so than I needed to be, probably because we'd been flying several hours already and I was stressed. He had a crestfallen look on his face.

Neither one of us said anything as I continued on with the sortie. After a couple minutes I had cooled down. Later we talked briefly about responsibilities when picking up a load. He still looked disheartened. I know he'd been feeling good about himself and his flying. He'd just been playing the cool pilot, talking to the guys on the ground. That kind of camaraderie could really feel good sometimes. He just wanted to fit in. *I'll have to make sure to tell him later that it's okay, everything is cool, he's doing a good job,* I thought to myself. But I didn't.

That evening I was tired so I didn't stay up very late. I did catch the flick and sip a couple beers during the movie. I was in a deep sleep when there was a KAWUMP! "Incoming!"

Before I fully came to consciousness, I was on the floor pulling my mattress over me as best I could. Sometime in the past couple months I had decided that my first response to a rocket attack would be to hunker down under my mattress on the floor, and then to decide how long I'd stay there before heading for the bunker. I heard guys running down the sidewalk. I stayed where I was and tried to gauge if there was regular time interval to the rocket impacts. There were several rounds, a couple sounded close. When they seemed to be less frequent, I got up and ran to the bunker. There we all stayed until it appeared there were no more incoming. Then we grabbed our weapons and went to our assigned revetments to guard the aircraft in case there was a penetration of the perimeter. We stayed there until we got an all clear. As always in such circumstances, my truncated night of sleep was not very restful.

The next morning we were checking out one of the aircraft revetments. A rocket had landed right at the base of the thick wall and had blown a large hole in it. However, we were all marveling that the Chinook parked there didn't have a mark on it, not a piece of shrapnel, nothing. That was one time a revetment really did what it was supposed to do — protect the aircraft.

I was back in the air that day and the next. Late in the afternoon of the thirteenth, after we'd returned to the Locker Room and shut down, I grabbed my gear and headed for my hootch, as usual. A few guys were hanging around outside the O Club, and one of them said, "101 went down at Fuller."

Incredulous, I asked, "What happened?"

"I guess they were on short final approach, just coming to a hover, when they took a direct hit from a mortar. The aircraft apparently just dropped right where they were going to set down their load. I think their load was fuel bladders. It burned right there."

"How about the crew?"

"I guess most of them had some pretty serious burns and other injuries but the guys on the ground got them out of there. Pendergast was the left door gunner. He didn't make it. Heard that the mortar hit right about where he was."

Any energy I still had in my body seemed to disappear. I felt so listless. I sat down.

"Who was the AC? Who was flying with him?"

"Bill Mayer. Heard that his helmet got blown clean off his head in the explosion. Les Parent was his pilot."

"Oscar ..." I said, mumbling the short version of his nickname, 'Oscar Mayer, the wiener magnate.' "Where are the guys now?"

"I guess a Dust-off picked 'em up and medivaced them to a hospital ship off the coast."

I just sat there and listened as the guys talked and speculated about this and that. This couldn't be happening again, but no one was denying it. I didn't know what to think. I didn't know Pendergast very well, but he was a fellow crew member, a Varsity comrade. Another mom and dad would never be the same. Did he have any brothers and sisters? A girlfriend? I felt bad that I didn't know. My mind was kind of hazy. I just couldn't figure it out ... two guys killed in less than a week. And now four WIAs. And a Chinook destroyed. It was kind of ironic that tail number 101 would go down. It had had a bit of celebrity, what with it assigned to the 101st. I had flown it several times. And now it was nothing more than ashes on Firebase Fuller. I didn't pray. I didn't know what to pray. Even if I found the words, would God even listen?

Robert Lee Pendergast, born Apr. 1, 1950...

Chapter 30

*…the dead, who had already died,
are happier than the living, who are
still alive.*

--Ecclesiastes 4:2 (NIV)

For some reason I didn't write Donna about the tragedies, the KIAs and the WIAs. It was without question that those stories would be left out of letters to Mom and Dad, but I didn't know why I wouldn't write about it to Donna. Usually I felt I could write her anything I wanted or needed to. She was a willing, compassionate listener, but I kept it to myself. I guess I just wanted to try to forget about it. Maybe I didn't want to think about the grief of their families back home when they got the news. But I didn't really know for sure.

*　　*　　*

16 Apr 70

Dear Donna,

　Guess what! Know what the big news is? I'm a "double digit midget!" That means I have less than 100 days to go! I just can't believe it! Won't be too long now. I'm looking forward especially to seeing you again. I've had so many dreams about that. I'm mainly looking forward to enjoying your companionship, just being with you, getting to know you...

*　　*　　*

20 Apr 70

Dear Donna,

　...Guess what I've been doing the whole month of April? Flying — every single day. We had three of our ACs (aircraft commanders) go home this month so we're really in a bind now. However, there are four guys who will be making AC shortly, so that will take the load off us a little. Actually, I don't really mind flying all the time because I've never had a

month go by as fast as April has. I don't get nearly so tired as I used to before I went on R & R, either. When I fly all the time, though, I don't have too much time for anything else, e.g., washing clothes. You see, the Vietnamese mama-sans we used to have doing our laundry can't be here anymore since some of them were suspected VC sympathizers...Know how I have to wash my clothes now? I put some water and soap in a little tub, then use my bare feet for an agitator. My hands work as a wringer. It's kinda funny to watch, but it does get the job done. That is one thing I'll never record on film.

The flare-up of action we had the past couple weeks is subsiding somewhat. This area is still a lot "hotter" than it was last fall. We divide most of our flying between working the mountains west of here and supporting the firebases up near the DMZ. I'd say that at least 50% of our work is done for the ARVNs...

*   *   *

26 Apr 70

Dear Donna,

It's a hot, sunny afternoon. The winds are real gusty, and thunderheads (cumulo-nimbus) are building high over the mountains. It's quite an injection of power, what with the elements of nature in turmoil. At least that's how I always view an afternoon thunderstorm which is brewing. I came down early in the afternoon [...] because most of the missions were already completed. There's a couple loads remaining which can't be flown because the firebase they are going to is partially socked in, and besides, the turbulence is too bad (the firebase is high in the mountains).

Speaking of heat, I really don't dare to tell you this, but [Phil and I] have an air conditioner now. Yup, you heard me right. I guess now I've lost what remnants of sympathy you had for my "tough" life. I never really have complained about my living conditions, though, have I? I live quite well, at least better than the grunts in the field. [We] got it from one of [our] buddies who just went home. So, now I can spend my last 90 days here in comfort. It was so great last night when I had to crawl <u>underneath</u> my blankets...[T]he best thing about an air conditioner is that the room is de-humidified...

Love, Dale

*　　　*　　　*

After finishing my letter to Donna, I went to get some chow, then to the club for our pilot's meeting. Captain Mike Dallas, our ops officer, surprised me by saying that I was grounded for the next four or five days. The maximum number of flying hours we were allowed to accumulate in a thirty-day period was 140 hours. I guess it was a safety consideration. Apparently I had passed that mark in about twenty-five days. I didn't mind a couple days off because I felt so exhausted. But after that I would just as soon get back in the cockpit. I wished I could've had a couple days off in the middle of the past twenty-five days. That would have made more sense.

Chapter 31

*Who of you by worrying
can add a single hour to his life?*

--Matthew 6:27 (NIV)

1 May 1970

It was another full day of flying, most of it in Quang Tri province which borders the DMZ on the north. I had another new guy flying with me, Phil Arnold, who'd been in country less than a month. He'd been doing a good job for being so new. I'd been trying my best to give him some experience to help acclimate him as quickly as possible.

Today was my sister Sharon's birthday. I'd blown that one—hadn't gotten a card in the mail for her. Hopefully she would understand. And tomorrow would be my birthday. I'd just finished my first full year of adulthood, and tomorrow I'd be hitting the ripe old age of twenty-two. I suspected I'd be "celebrating" with another full day of missions. Oh well, time went faster that way. Less than ninety days to go now.

I was starting to notice that I was a little more on edge lately. I was worrying about taking hits, something which normally didn't cross my mind for days or even weeks at a time. And when I'd crawl into bed, the thought of getting rocketed that night would be front and center in my mind. More than once I would start wondering whether I'd "get it" with mere days or weeks to go after having survived intact for over nine months in country. I tried to laugh it off as a bit of short-timer's paranoia, but deep down I couldn't shake it.

I was feeling exceptionally weary at the end of this day as we set down at the Camp Eagle refueling pad en route to the Locker Room. It was already past the normal dinner time at the chow hall, but there'd be some food for us. The sun was getting low over the mountains to the west. I was just relieved that the day was coming to an end. I needed some rest. I made my obligatory call to operations: "Ops, this is 020, we're refueling and will be at the Locker Room shortly."

"Uh, negative 020," Mike responded. "We just got a mission add-on for a priority load to Ripcord."

Before thinking, I mashed my transmit button and yelled into my mike: "No way! We've been flying all day and we're wiped out! Find someone else who's still out there flying!"

There was a momentary pause, then: "Fine! I'll just tell battalion that my pilots won't fly the mission!"

I started to say something, then caught myself. I sat there, thought it through, then sighed: "Okay, what ya got?"

After we were given the particulars of the mission, I told the crew we were going back out. "Okay, Phil, you got it for this sortie."

After we picked up our sling load, we headed west to the mountains and Firebase Ripcord. It was a beautiful evening over the rugged terrain, deep shadows were forming as the sun dipped lower in the western sky. But I didn't notice it like I usually did because I was still feeling rather angry and put upon. I just wanted to get this last mission over and put this sucker on the ground.

By the time we got to Ripcord, the sun had set and we were in twilight. Yellow smoke marked the spot where the firebase wanted the load. Phil had initiated his descent and was steep on his approach. I motioned "down" with my hand. Apparently Phil didn't understand my hand signal (which, in retrospect, I don't think anyone would have understood) and looked uncertainly at me: "What do you want me to do?"

"You're high. Bring it down."

The aircraft continued down but not enough and remained too high.

"I've got it," I said brusquely, none too kindly. I pulled in power and initiated a go-around. Instead of using this as a teaching moment and explaining what I was doing and why, I said nothing other than curtly telling Pathfinder Ripcord we were going around. I was quite sure Phil was embarrassed and feeling down. I came around, set up my approach, and brought the load onto the firebase. After releasing it, I took off, rapidly gained a lot of altitude, and pointed her east.

"Okay, take us home."

As I sat there quietly smoking a cigarette, I felt a lot of the resentment and tension drain away. I started feeling sorry for Phil and rather miffed with myself for the way I handled the situation. Finally I broke the silence.

"You know, you sure don't want your approach to be too low in the mountains, especially when there's a lot of wind because you could get caught in a downdraft. At the same time, if you're too high, you'll need to pull in more power to bring it to a hover over the firebase. If you max out your power, there's a real possibility you may fall through. There's a narrow band for safe approaches, especially in the mountains."

He nodded, "Yeah, I guess I just need to get some more experience."

I was going to tell him he was doing fine, give him some positive strokes, but it was time to call Eagle Tower.

After I dropped my gear in my hootch, I went to the club and checked for mail on the pool table before going to get some chow. Not only were there letters and cards, there was a package. I dropped the mail off, quickly got something to eat, then came back to my room to open the mail. The package was from Donna and was for my birthday. It was filled with what I most appreciated in care packages—baked goods. In no time I had downed five or more cookies. I opened what I was pretty sure was a birthday card. It was, and I slowly read through it, twice. It was obvious that Donna had taken it to several classes in school and had gotten a lot of her friends and teachers to sign it. For some reason it really hit me and humbled me. Here were all these people who didn't know me from Adam, and they were writing things like, "Hurry home," and "We're thinking of you." I thought I was going to lose it. I brushed some moisture from my eyes. I thought I was just very tired. I was going to write Donna and thank her before I got in bed.

Chapter 32

From birth I have relied on you;
you brought me forth from my mother's
womb...

--Psalm 71:6 (NIV)

2 May 1970

I'd actually made it to age twenty-two. Being a teenager seemed like such a long time ago. It was a grand, relaxing birthday. I flew ten solid hours again, and they were hectic ones to boot. Nothing more relaxing than that. My butt was numb, but at least I hadn't gotten any late add-on missions. I did enjoy a couple of cold beers and a movie. I polished off the rest of my cookies—felt rather gluttonous about it, but they tasted so good. What I really craved, though, was some sleep.

I tried reading a little but kept nodding off. I crawled into my rack and was out about the time my head hit the pillow.

KAWUMP!! KAWUMP!! Before I gained consciousness, I was already struggling to get under my bed and pulling my mattress on top of me. I was gasping for breath and my heart was racing. The 122-mm rockets seemed to be raining down. Explosion after explosion. Some seemed close. Then an extra close KAWUMP!!! And I could feel the concussion. Falling objects and the shattering sounds of breaking glass on our floor. My body jumped. The back of my neck turned clammy and cold. My gut churned. I tried to pull my mattress closer around me. I wanted to run to the bunker, but I knew there was broken glass on the floor. The rocket impacts were too close together.

Then it was quiet. I stayed where I was but pulled my boots on. I noticed a bit of a red glow coming from somewhere. I decided to run for the bunker. Glass crunched under my boots. I felt some relief when I ducked into the bunker. Most of the guys were in there. A cacophony of voices. Soon we were poking our heads out the door, then moving outside. The sky was turning a sickly yellowish red. Some of us hopped up on the bunker and from that vantage spot could see a couple fires raging. One looked to be in the Toros' company area next-door to us. Out in the southern sky beyond the perimeter, a couple Cobra gunships were working over an area, perhaps the area someone thought had been the source of the rockets. We figured Chuck was already long gone by now though. The rapid fire from their mini-guns, at a rate of six thousand rounds per minute, sounded like a chainsaw. "Yeah, go get 'em, get 'em!" some voices cheered them on.

Soon we were directed to get our steel pots, flak vests and weapons, and "guard" our assigned revetments and aircraft. My duty position gave me a front seat view of the conflagration in the Toros' company area. Suddenly the blaze seemed to blow up to triple its size as the color orange billowed skyward. This was accompanied by a sound more like a "whoosh" than an explosion. We figured a fuel bladder had just blown. I could see silhouettes of individuals trying to drag their Cobra gunships away from the flames. One of the parked Toro helicopters was too close to the fire, so the ground personnel backed away from it. It didn't take long for that Cobra to be engulfed in the fireworks. It burned fiercely; I ducked at the sound of secondary explosions. Their ammo dump went up as well, and 2.75-inch folding fin rockets and other rounds were cooking off. I was scared and yet transfixed by this terrible, other-worldly spectacle.

Later we found out that seven rockets had hit on our flight line. One rocket had gone off twenty yards from our living area. It so happened that it had landed in the middle of our little creek, so all it had done was blow a huge crater in the soft mud. That was the rocket that had provided us our broken glass. Besides that, my only other casualty was my radio—part of the antenna had broken off. Three of our aircraft had been damaged. The Toros, on the other hand, weren't so fortunate—their hangar, four aircraft and ammo dump had all been completely destroyed.

And with that, my twenty-second birthday in Vietnam was over.

*   *   *

3 May 70

Dear Donna,

...The action continues hot and heavy around here. Charlie is getting braver, attacking firebases, patrols, and shooting at all kinds of aircraft. Don't worry about me—I'm just fine. Charlie is paying dearly for his boldness. What it all proves, I'll never know. They kill us and we kill them. No one gains anything.

And now we're in Cambodia. I just sat and shook my head when I heard that on the radio. Nixon tells us we'll go in, destroy them, and pull back in six weeks. They told us something very similar five years ago when we came into Nam. Guess what. We're still here. We were just nicely disengaging ourselves from here, and then Tricky Dick blows his cool. Sure, if we are going to fight a war, let's hit their supply points, headquarters, and staging areas. But with the number of troops we have here, we're just spread too thin and the Commies are too well entrenched and hidden. To effectively fight this war we'd need twice or more than [...] the 500,000 we had here before. But since that'll never happen, let's get out of here instead of unnecessarily killing thousands more. No, I'm no pacifist by any means. But I like to think I'm a rational being, and [that] the way things are now is senselessness. We're killing them and they're killing us and nothing is gained. Don't let anyone tell you the gooks are good guys and their purpose is noble. No way. But we are wrong in sending thousands of our guys to their deaths year after year without accomplishing anything. I would like nothing more than to see the Vietnamese a free people, free to choose for themselves, free to find hope for their future. Well, now that I put you in a thoroughly great mood with all my happy news...

I've been getting the usual, welcome, beautiful flow of mail from you. It keeps me going and keeps my spirits up...

Yup, we still have our cookouts. Hardly miss a Saturday with the steaks, occasional beer, etc...It's a lot of fun and gives us something to look forward to every week. 'Course, I have only about ten more cookouts to look forward to!

Take care, and I'll see you soon!

Love, Dale

*   *   *

Platte, South Dakota

circa May 1962

I never liked it when Dad was gone and there was weather like this. He was away serving as a delegate at our denomination's Board of Trustees meetings in Grand Rapids, Michigan. I always felt somewhat safer when Dad was home and the weather forecasters were issuing watches and warnings. This afternoon it was a tornado watch. Again.

The sky looked creepy; the atmosphere was strange and ominous. Heavy, sullen cloud masses rose thousands of feet into the air. I would look for more wind, but instead we'd get a gust, then silence. A weird shade of green was developing in the clouds. I pedaled my bike faster and got my newspapers delivered in record time. I felt some relief when I arrived home.

Mom seemed her usual calm self. I wished she would pay more attention to the weather like Dad did. She seemed almost oblivious to what was going on outside. I decided I needed to raise the alarm. Don pitched in and expressed his concerns as well. But she only responded with further calm: "We'll be fine. There's no need to get all worried."

Okay, I guess Don and I would just have to take responsibility for standing vigilant.

We ate supper at our usual time, in our usual way. Afterward Don and I went out back. The sky was still as threatening as before. "It's gonna hail," Don said, having noted the green tint in the clouds. A sudden strong wind surged through the trees. A little rain began to fall, then stopped as quickly as it had begun. Soon there was a rattle of hail hitting the back yard, forcing us to take shelter on the porch.

The hail lasted for only a few seconds. We went back outside. The wind died down to nothing. Eerie silence. Then in the distance we could hear a muffled roaring sound, getting louder, as if a large freight train were approaching. To the southwest we could now see clouds boiling up over the trees.

"Tornado!" Don yelled. Just then a siren started to wail.

We ran into the house. "Tornado! Get downstairs to the storm cellar!" We quickly gathered up all the kids and headed downstairs. Off of our basement was the storm cellar, a small, dank underground room with a convex ceiling of thick cement. It also served as a passageway to the outside from the basement—the cellar, also called a tornado shelter, had a horizontal door over one end which opened into our backyard. There was a wooden door between the main basement room and the cellar. When we tried to open the door, we found it was stuck. I yanked on the door but it wouldn't budge. Because of a prolonged spell of wet weather, the door had probably swelled a bit. I felt panic rising in my gut.

"Where's Mom?" Don asked. We looked around—we had everyone there except Mom. Don ran upstairs yelling for Mom. I kept pulling on the door to no avail.

In less than a minute Mom came down the steps. "Don, I can't get this door open!" I shouted. Just then it gave way and opened. I felt immense relief as we all immediately moved into the shelter.

"Mom, where were you?" I asked.

"Oh, just on the front porch watching the storm."

"But there's a tornado coming!"

"It didn't look so bad. We're all okay now."

I was exasperated with Mom and her casual demeanor toward the storm. Yet I was so grateful that we had our family together in the safest part of the house. The winds were howling outside, and I cringed expectantly for the sounds of destruction. At the same time I felt strangely comforted by the cocoon of the shelter.

We waited for a few minutes. There was no telling what the situation was outside. Then Don said, "I'm gonna to see what's going on out there."

"Don't you go outside now!" Mom warned.

But Don already had the door to the backyard open and was looking around as he stood on the steps. "Nothing happening right here. I'm going outside."

A moment later I got up the nerve to follow him out. "You boys be careful," said Mom anxiously.

"Oh, man, look at that!" Don yelled.

I moved to where he was standing which gave us a clear view of the farmlands west of town. I caught my breath when I saw what he was looking at—less than a mile from town was a large black cloud with a classic funnel reaching down and connecting with the earth. I stood mesmerized as the twister worked its way north. It appeared that its course would keep it away from town. We watched it approach a farmhouse with a barn and a few smaller buildings. Then a swirl of dust and cloud obscured the farm. As the funnel slowly continued on its way, a horrible realization made its way into my consciousness—the farm we'd been looking at was gone: no farmhouse, no barn, no buildings, nothing. Where just a few moments before a farm had interrupted the prairie's horizon, there was now a smooth, uninterrupted line between fields and sky. I felt a cold wave pulse through my body, even though the ambient temperature had not changed. Boards and other wreckage were clearly visible, being pulled up into the heart of the tornado's funnel. I saw a streamer, maybe a roll of toilet paper, winding round and round the rotating twister. As the tornado continued on its path of destruction, the funnel and part of its parent cloud turned suddenly from black to almost white. We figured it had gone over a small lake that was in the vicinity and had sucked a massive amount of water into its swirling mass.

Don ran into the house to get his camera. Mom and the younger kids came out of the house about the same time he did. He ran across the street to the north and climbed up onto the roof of Bergeson's Machine Shop. About that time the funnel started pulling up from the ground and continued upward until it disappeared into the cloud formation. Don was still on Bergeson's roof with camera in hand, motioning for the funnel to come down again. But after watching for a few more minutes, it appeared the tornado had wreaked all the desolation it would for that day.

Our electricity was off. As it got dark, I decided to go downtown (only a short city block away), to see if the power was out there as well. Main Street was dark. Jagged streaks of lightning filled the sky – the cloud-to-cloud lightning racked the sky almost continuously. There was little if any audible thunder. The atmosphere seemed very alien, and I felt a deep dread inside of me. I noticed a gathering by the fire station so I walked over. Our town fire truck had been pulled out of the station, and some of the town fathers were attempting to establish some communication with its two-way radio. I couldn't hear much of the responses they were getting due to the static of the radio. I didn't like the deep concern etched on their faces. I walked slowly away. The lightning continued in the skies. I wished Dad were home. Was this the way the world would come to an end?

Chapter 33

…[Lord], I…believe;
help me overcome my unbelief!

--Mark 9:24 (NIV)

5 May 1970

It was promotion day for me. Actually, it wasn't that big a deal because it was virtually automatic, after spending a year as a WO-1. It had been one year ago that I'd been sworn in as an officer. The following day (6 May 1969) had been graduation day from flight school, when I had gotten my wings. What a lot had happened since then! While the promotion itself wasn't that big a deal, the effect it had in my paycheck was welcome—a nice little raise was awaiting me. So I became a CWO (Chief Warrant Officer), or more specifically a CW-2.

As usual we'd been flying a lot. And since the sun was coming up earlier, we were being awakened earlier so we could take off at first light to better enable us to get all our missions completed, especially with the increased workload. That earlier wake-up was now at 3:50 a.m. Of course that allowed time for dressing, eating breakfast, checking out the missions, and pre-flight inspections of the aircraft.

I came down for the day in the early afternoon. The helicopter I'd been flying was due for a periodic maintenance, so I was grateful to have a good part of the afternoon off. I sat down in the shade by the O Club for awhile to shoot the breeze with some of the guys.

It felt good to kick back and just do nothing but listen to unimportant chatter about who knows what. As the voices droned on, I dozed off a couple times. Then I saw Mike, the ops officer, rushing around the corner toward us. The look on his face caused an involuntary tightening of my muscles. "435's been shot down! Everyone's dead! There's no survivors."

"Huh?" "What?" a couple voices sounded at the same time.

"Little George, Richard Van De Warker, Larry Buffington, Gary Brown, Steve Wasson, they're all dead. Shot down. Burned."

My body turned cold. I was having trouble making sense out of what Mike had just said. I couldn't focus, felt light-headed, sweating.

"Where?"

"About due west of Camp Evans. In the foothills. They had a sling load."

I slumped in my chair. I didn't even want to hear any more. Two fellow pilots. Friends. And three more crew members. Dead. I wouldn't see them in the mess hall that night. Not at the Gork watching a movie. Little George with a chaw of tobacco in his cheek, trying to look tough, a bit of a swagger ... I guess they did that in Oklahoma. Not even twenty-one years old yet. He had such a baby face — looked like a high schooler. Just a kid. I used to laugh at George some, and I used to laugh *with* George a lot. Not anymore. I'd never see him again. Ever.

And Richard — I'd hit him once not too long ago. I could still see the stunned look on his face, just as vividly as if I was still in that cockpit. *Oh, God, why'd I do that? Why didn't I tell him everything was okay, that he was doing* good? Can't now. Never. I could have told him. Didn't. Too busy. Doing what?

I didn't like the feeling that was inside of me. But what could I do? Nothing. Maybe I could pray. But I didn't even know how to start. What would I say? What difference would it make? The guys would still be dead. I didn't want that to be real, wanted to think of something different. But I couldn't.

God, please help me. I don't know what I want you to do. I feel like crap, and I'd like it to go away. ...Are you even there? ...Sometimes I wonder if God is really real. Does he even exist? Maybe not here in Nam. Maybe for some reason he's just washed his hands of this place. I don't know – I can't even think of what I do know. ...But that would be illogical. If he exists at all, he would be here in Nam, too. Otherwise he wouldn't be God. And I really think he is real. My mom and dad taught me that from as far back as I can remember. And I believe it... I'm just having a hard time understanding what's going on. ...I wish this would stop. I wish I could go home now.

Chapter 34

And just as you saw the iron mixed
with baked clay,
so the people will be a mixture and
will not remain united,
any more than iron mixes with clay.

--Daniel 2:43 (NIV)

6 May 1970

We didn't get rocketed last night. After breathing a sigh of relief, I remembered that it would be well over two months before I would catch my Freedom Bird back to the world. I just needed to stop thinking every night about the possibility of getting rocketed.

Today was a no-fly day for me. I had recon (reconnaissance) patrol this morning, a duty we pulled every few months. After breakfast, I got my steel pot and flak jacket and met the six guys for the patrol that I'd be leading. One of the men had an M-79 grenade launcher, and the rest of the patrol were armed with M-16 rifles. One member also carried a PRC-25 radio. We got a quick intel briefing from a captain in the command post. We were told to go outside the perimeter about a half mile or so and check for anything that looked suspicious with the Vietnamese hootches. We were also supposed to check for signs of enemy activity in the groves of trees and rice paddies, such as footprints close to the perimeter, hidden ammo, mortar aiming sticks, etc. I rated the chances of us finding anything like that about zero. I'd rather have been flying, but I wasn't given that option.

After the briefing, we headed for the perimeter and went through the wire. To be honest, I actually found these infrequent forays somewhat interesting. It gave me a chance to see up close, rather than from the air, how some of the locals lived. Most of the structures close to the perimeter were abandoned. They looked very plain and simple. The terrain was a beautiful lush green though, especially the few rice paddies we saw. Other than a couple mama-sans, we saw no adults.

Kids were another matter. It wasn't long before we encountered a dozen or so boys, most of whom seemed to be eight to ten years old. When they saw us, they ran up to us, everyone talking at once: "Hey, G.I., give me cigarette!" "Hey, G.I., give me chocolate!" They were laughing and smiling and seemed to be having a good time, not a care in the world. Some of us had saved chocolate bars from our C-ration boxes for the occasion.

A couple guys gave mini-lectures on children smoking: "Cigarettes no good, number ten. Make you sick. You no grow up to be big and strong."

"No, no, cigarettes number one, good for me," replied a smiling face.

I didn't give out any smokes. I figured it was bad enough that I indulged, but I sure didn't want a young growing boy to get hooked on tobacco. More than one of our patrol passed out a cigarette here and there. I didn't stop them. In a few seconds about half a dozen kids were puffing away like old pros. I guess they were already hooked.

In no time the kids were merrily on their way. "Hey, G.I., you number one!" we heard as they departed. As I watched them go, it occurred to me that these kids were more like kids back home than not.

Thankfully it was a normal patrol without any activity. We headed back through the wire. I told the guys to go back to the company area while I debriefed the intel officer. I told him what we'd encountered, which was basically nothing. As I left the command post I knew I'd be back in a few hours—I had been stuck with the role of officer of the guard for our sector of the perimeter tonight. That's another extra duty we pulled every few months. One good thing—I would most likely have to do that only once more before going home.

After I got rid of my weapon, pot, and flak jacket, it was time for the chow hall. The menu typically was meat and potatoes, whether it was the noon meal or the evening. However, more often than not I ate C's for lunch as I flew. Halfway to the chow hall I decided I'd wait for evening to get my meat and potatoes. I went back to my hootch, got out a spaghetti and meat sauce LRRP ration, boiled some water, and poured the water over the dried food. In a few minutes I had a hydrated, hot meal which tasted better than a lot of chow hall food, and much better than C's. But it was harder to lay hands on LRRPs, so I tended to treasure them when I had them.

After lunch I kicked back and did a little reading, then moseyed over to the club to see if anyone was hanging around. The mail had come, as had the daily *Stars and Stripes*. As usual, I had mail—not one, but two letters from Donna. Instead of taking my mail to my hootch to read as I usually did, I ripped into them as I sat by the club, then slowly read them through, savoring each and every word.

As my DEROS was getting closer, I had started having concerns again regarding which direction our relationship would take once we were together in the States, and I had written to Donna about them. In one of the letters I read today she had responded to those concerns. Basically she relieved many of my anxieties. I felt a renewed excitement about seeing her again, and spending lots of time with her. Of course we still didn't know exactly what the nature of our relationship would be, but now I dared to dream about a beautiful future. She had been such a sweetheart while I'd been in Nam, so important in keeping my morale up, just in being there for me through her letters, always with such an upbeat tone. Even if we were to part ways as "just" friends, I would be forever grateful to her for what she had meant to me this past year.

I turned my attention to the half dozen or so guys who were gathered by the club. They were talking about what had happened at Kent State University in Ohio a couple days ago. I had heard about it on AFVN. Apparently there were major demonstrations against the war going on all over the US—which was nothing new—after units south of us went into Cambodia. The Ohio governor had activated the National Guard to keep order at Kent State. I didn't know if the demonstrations were worse or more dangerous there than in other places. For some unknown reason some of the Guard troops opened fire on the students, wounding several, but worst of all killing four. I simply couldn't understand that. There was more than enough shooting going on over here. We'd just lost Little George and crew yesterday. But now

233

we were fighting each other? We're all Americans, for crying out loud. We don't have to agree, but we sure shouldn't be killing each other. With all that I'd been hearing, I was eager to read an article about Kent State in today's *Stars and Stripes*, but it didn't answer many questions.

I refocused on the bull session by the club. The conversation was getting more animated as opinions were expressed about Kent State. Mike, our ops officer, was stating his frustration about the shootings: "They're just kids."

In response, Joe, a civilian technical representative for a Department of Defense-related corporation, commented loudly: "They're a bunch of snot-nosed punks who have no clue what's going on over here and got what was coming to them!"

Then several voices were raised, everyone seemed upset or angry. I don't know how many, if any, felt like I did. It seemed as if whatever held us together as a people was coming apart at the seams. My world seemed to be turning upside down, and I felt discombobulated. Yet I had two letters in my hand which were the very antithesis of what I felt. I decided I'd had enough and just went to my hootch. I re-read my letters and tried to keep my focus on them instead of what was going on around me. I needed to rest awhile before spending the night awake in the command post. I lay on my rack and tried to relax. I wasn't able to.

After dinner in the chow hall, I reported to the command post. I hated the thought of another long night sitting in that grungy control room. I decided to check the guys on the perimeter a couple extra times tonight, to make extra sure they stayed awake, but also to keep myself awake. I wasn't going to tolerate any sleeping on the line, so I couldn't tolerate it in myself. With as much bad guy activity as we'd had in our AO, guarding the perimeter was serious business.

The twelve hours trickled by at an agonizingly slow pace, but eventually came to an end. Thankfully it was a quiet night, and I didn't catch anyone sleeping. Maybe all the coffee helped, but most of the guys seemed pretty serious about their duty as well. I went to my hootch and fell fast asleep.

Chapter 35

Worship the Lord with gladness...

--Psalm 100:2 (NIV)

10 May 70

Dear Donna,

...[H]ave a day off today. I went to chapel services which I really appreciated. Today was the first time in over three months that I've been to services...We can always worship our God in our hearts, but it's not quite like going to services specifically for that purpose. I feel much more restful now, like a lot of my problems and cares have been taken away. It is a much closer feeling when you have a group of Christians gathered for the same purpose. I feel that this is just a little taste of what heaven will be like.

Well, let's see now. Is it 74 days, or is it 10 ½ weeks, or is it 2 ½ months? Have your pick. But anyway you look at it, I'm getting "short!" I'm starting to have visions of a Boeing 707 lifting off the runway of Cam Ranh Bay (where I leave from) and setting down at Mc Chord AFB, near Seattle. It's kinda funny, but I'll get there about the same time [and day] I leave. Washington's time is 15 hours behind here, and it's about a 15-hour trip... That's okay with me because then I won't lose any leave time.

Oh, yes, I got my orders for my next assignment. I'll be going to Ft. Benning, GA, which makes me just a little disappointed. I had wanted to go to Ft. Rucker and be an I.P. (instructor pilot), but I'd better forget about that now...[Ft. Benning has] an aviation unit that I'm going to, which has a few Chinooks and Hueys. They are used mainly for administration purposes and in [...] training guys who are going through OCS, NCO Academy, and Ranger School at Ft. Benning. I've got a feeling things will be boring with not much to do. Oh well, I'll only have 15 months left in the Army when I get home…

I can't believe you've never heard of "double digit midget" before. Why, that's universal language around here. Before you know it, I'll be a "60 day loss" (less than 60 days to go)…

…Take care; won't be long now.

Love, Dale

*   *   *

14 May 70

Dear Donna,

Can you believe it? Seven zero days! Yup, 70 days. I really can't believe it. I betcha this [is getting] boring, me talking about how many days I have left and saying the same thing over and over, but it's really the most exciting thing I have to talk about. I still can't believe that I've been here this long. Seems like such a short time ago that I was saying my goodbyes last summer. I hope I never have to go through something like that again. I hate saying goodbye. I can hardly take looking into a person's eyes when saying goodbyes…

Oh, I think I forgot to tell you, but do you know what we had at our weekly barbecue last Saturday? It wasn't just the regular old steaks. We had <u>T-bone</u> steaks and lobster tails! I'm not really a lobster nut, but really grooved out on that T-bone. And we had some potato salad and other good stuff to go with it. I know, I know, what a way to fight a war.

We've been busy supporting the same old firebases, as usual. We still divide our time between the DMZ area and the mountains to the west. We haven't gone into the Ashau Valley yet, but we aren't too very far from it. The bad guys have been *relatively quiet, but they still like to shoot at helicopters and also base camps with rockets and mortars.*

...Glad you are getting nice weather. And graduation is almost here. No, I can't understand all the shutting down of schools and campuses because of Cambodia. So many students who really want an education are really being hurt, especially at the schools that are closed for the rest of the term. There's so many things I don't understand anymore...

I know I don't always say it, but I want to thank you for all the many beautiful letters you write to me. I appreciate them all so very much. They make me warm, brighten my life, and always give me something to look forward to. Please believe me that you have made this whole tour so much more bearable, that you made life look brighter. Thank you for all this.

Please take care now. I will see you soon.

Love, Dale

Chapter 36

Then the LORD answered Job out of the storm...
'Who is this that darkens my counsel with words without knowledge?
...Will the one who contends with the Almighty correct him?
Let him who accuses God answer him!'

--Job 38:1-2; 40:2 (NIV)

17 May 1970

Another early wake-up. It would be another full day if the weather held. This was supposed to be the "dry" season now, but that only meant that most of our precipitation came from an afternoon build-up of thunderstorms rather than the all-day rains of the monsoons. Plus, temps were usually over 100° with sweltering humidity during the dry season. The monsoon season tended to be much cooler during the cloudy days.

One of our first missions looked to be unique — the only information the mission sheet showed was that we needed to go to a particular supply point to pick up a chem officer who would brief us on our mission. As we arrived at the supply point and my pilot brought the aircraft to a hover, I noticed a couple of black G.I.s about one hundred yards to our left front. I stuck my left arm out my side window and gave them a "black power" salute, wagging my fist in the air. They got big smiles on their faces and returned my salute. I couldn't help smiling myself. Maybe I had made a connection, however small, in spite of society's racial divisions.

After we had set down on the PSP and shut down, the chem guy who'd been waiting for us introduced himself and explained the mission.

"We'll be loading drums of powdered CS gas in the back of the Chinook. We'll then be flying over part of the Ho Chi Minh trail and dropping the drums of gas onto the trail. The idea is to make it unusable or at least more difficult to use for the NVA. As you probably know, the Ho Chi Minh trail is not really a single trail but a series of trails; but where we're going you'll be able to see that there is one trail that stands out. We'll be up in the far northwest corner of South Vietnam." He indicated that this mission had been done previously, more than once.

We'd been supporting firebases in that general area, but this mission took us beyond our normal AO. I was glad we'd be having a couple of Cobra gunships as escorts. I had my doubts about the effectiveness of the mission, but I didn't know enough about CS gas to really have any basis for my doubts. My only exposure had been during boot camp. As with tear gas, we got to breathe it for a few seconds before escaping the "gas chamber." My memory was that it was much stronger and nastier than tear gas—I remember thinking that if I had to take one more breath of CS, I was going to die. Of course, no one did. Anyway it didn't seem like it would be that tough for the bad guys, as resourceful as the NVA were, to simply bypass the drop areas if in fact the gas had any effect and staying power. Besides, they probably had gas masks. But as the old Army adage goes, "Ours is not to reason why, ours is but to do or die."

After we were loaded with CS drums and had joined up with our snake escorts, we headed up the coastal plain for awhile, then proceeded over the rugged mountains to the northwest. Usually our cruising altitude was between 1500 and 2000 feet AGL, but today's mission would be flown at 5000 feet AGL. According to intel, the bad guys had plenty of heavier automatic weapons in that area, especially .51-caliber machine guns. I couldn't help marveling at the glorious beauty of this wild mountainous country, although it was pockmarked in many places from bombs and artillery. My body shivered at the thought of going down in that triple canopy jungle, deep in some nameless ravine. Would this be my fate, with a mere two months of my tour to go? *Okay, knock off the paranoia*, I thought to myself. The further we flew, the more it became like a no-man's land — there were just no signs of any civilization. We were definitely in Indian country again.

"Our initial point is about five minutes straight ahead. When we reach it we'll follow the trail to the southeast," the chem guy said from his perch on the jump seat. He got up and went to the cargo compartment to check that his guys, who'd been brought along for the purpose of rolling the drums out the back of the Chinook, were ready.

Soon a relatively broad valley came into view. Almost everything was a deep green thanks to the heavy vegetation, but there was a distinctive stripe of reddish brown running from northwest to southeast.

"That's our target."

The chem officer was right — that road did stand out very clearly. From our altitude it looked like it was graded gravel or dirt, in good shape for vehicles, although we didn't see any.

"Okay, what works best is to put that road right between your foot pedals and just follow it that way, straight and level, around eighty knots."

As we got lined up and started down the trail, he directed his troops to start dropping the drums. I concentrated on keeping the aircraft over the road. Every once in awhile, I glanced around to take in the view, mesmerized by the wild beauty of the long valley.

"We're right on target," came the voice of the chem guy over the intercom. "I've seen several of the drums hit smack dab on the road. Keep doing what you're doing."

A short time later, the right door gunner yelled into his mike: "Sir, we're taking fire!"

"Can you tell where it's coming from?"

"Looks to be from our four or five o'clock. I can't see anything on the ground. All I can see are the tracer rounds. They look to be arcing under us. Man, those tracers look as big as basketballs!"

Our pilot quickly relayed the info to our Cobra escorts. "Okay, Varsity, we'll go take a look and see if we can find anything." A couple minutes later the snake leader came back on the horn: "They must have fired a burst or two and then dee-deed. Lots of .51s in this area."

"Okay, thanks. Given the size of the tracers, it probably was .51s."

In a couple minutes, the last of the gas drums had been rolled out the back end, and we were headed back to civilization to drop off our chem guests. When we came out of the mountains and were over the coastal plains, our gunship escorts radioed us and said they were breaking off.

"Okay, thanks much for your help. By the way, do you have a pilot in your unit with the initials echo, alpha, papa (E.A.P.)?" I said. We weren't allowed to say proper names over the air.

"Yeah, we sure do."

"Would you tell him hello from Pete? We were classmates in flight school."

"Roger that. Will do."

The mission to the Ho Chi Minh trail took the better part of the morning. The rest of our missions for that day consisted of humping loads to firebases in the mountains in the vicinity of the Ashau Valley further south. I ate some cold Cs for lunch while my pilot flew a sortie. There was a noticeable build-up of clouds to our north already in early afternoon. The clouds in the area we'd been working weren't much of a factor yet, and I didn't think they'd keep us from flying our sorties today. As usual, the turbulence over the mountains was bouncing us around quite a bit—more shake, rattle and roll than I would have chosen if it had been up to me.

By the time we had dropped off our last load, it was late afternoon and we were on our way home, by way of the Camp Eagle refueling pad. The pain in the butt I felt had become all too common on these long days of flying. I was ready for a cold beer, a decent meal, and a shower.

After we had shut down in the Locker Room and filled out our flight log, my pilot and I grabbed our gear and headed for the officer's living area. A few guys were sitting around by the club which was pretty much the norm for this time of the day. When their general demeanor registered in my brain, I felt an involuntary shudder run through my body. I immediately became wary. Hopefully all it amounted to was more arguing about Kent State or anti-war demonstrations in general. I felt like leaving on my chicken plate.

"What's going on?"

No one said anything for a moment.

"497 went down this afternoon. Shot down. Crashed and burned. No survivors."

This couldn't be happening again. I sat down. My gut tightened up so much I felt like I was having trouble breathing.

"Apparently they were on a weather check northwest of Evans. Low ceiling."

Damn weather checks! I hated them! They were so unnecessary! If there was a low ceiling, take our word for it! Let us come home or at least stay on the ground at Evans. No way would we be able to get into a mountain firebase at a higher elevation if the ceiling in the lowlands was low. And now someone gets killed. Stupid! Stupid! Stupid!

"Who?"

"Big George, Phil Arnold, Roy Petty. Heard a rumor they'd gotten a radio transmission off, that they were taking fire and Petty had been hit, but I guess that was it."

Another voice said, "Sammy Alexander and Dave Smith were the other two crew members."

I didn't want to hear anymore—didn't want to stay there. I couldn't believe this was real, but I had no information to give me any hope that it wasn't. How could this be happening? Two birds. Two whole crews. Two weeks apart. Less than two weeks apart? We couldn't keep going like this.

I just sat there for awhile, looking at the ground. I didn't say anything. No one did. Suddenly I got up, grabbed my flight gear and went to my hootch. I couldn't stand the stillness anymore. Maybe I'd go to the PX. What would I buy if I went? I didn't know what they had. Maybe I'd go to the chow hall. I felt like I was going to puke. Maybe I'd just lie on my bed for awhile.

No more Big George. George Schultz. If he wasn't the old man of the pilots, he was close to it. Thirty-one years old. Already had gray hair. New England accent, from Massachusetts. Good-natured old cuss. He was on his second tour in Nam. He wasn't married, I think he had a couple sisters.

And Phil Arnold. Married. Didn't know if he had any kids. He hadn't been in country even two months yet. Why had I been such a jerk to him on that mission late one day? Why didn't I apologize, or at least tell him it was okay, that he was doing good. But I didn't. Now I never would. I'd have to live with it now. Just like Van

De Warker. Hit Vandy. Didn't tell him things were cool. Now I never will.

God, I'm really angry now. Don't you think we've had enough now? Don't you think twelve guys from our outfit are more than our fair share? I don't know what to say. I want it to stop now. No more. I don't want to talk anymore. I don't want to pray. I'm done with it ... Who am I to be angry with God? ... I don't think I'm angry. But I think I feel angry. I just don't know. I don't know what's going on in my gut. ...I just think I'm very sad.

* * *

31 May 70

Dear Donna,

I suppose you are wondering where this letter has been. It's really quite simple: I just didn't get it written. I haven't written anything for about ten days now. I'm groping around for an excuse, but I don't really have any that are too good. I'm just getting to be a poor letter writer.

All I've known lately is work, eat, and sleep. Our wake-up time is anywhere between 3:50 and 4:30 a.m., and to tell you the truth, it's starting to get to me...about all [I] feel like doing is taking a shower and "shooting the bull" over a couple beers before falling on [my] bed to a restless night's sleep. What really gets me is every once in awhile those nights get interrupted by Charlie's rockets. You don't get much sleep those nights. Oh yes, we [flew] a couple dawn combat assaults last week which meant up at 3 a.m.

I just noticed by the date that yesterday was Memorial Day. I wonder how many people thought about the [twelve buddies and fellow crew members] I've lost out of this company in the last 1½ months. I didn't even really think about it. See how crudely a war can affect a person? It's sickening. "And all those who were left went about their business..."

Much love, Dale

Chapter 37

A little sleep, a little slumber,
a little folding of the hands to rest…

--Proverbs 24:33 (NIV)

6 June 1970

I woke up thinking about a nice break I'd had a few weeks ago. It had been in the middle of a stretch of very heavy flying, day after day. I'd been told to get some things together because I was going to Saigon to pick up a new aircraft. I hadn't argued a bit: this would be a much appreciated break. A flight engineer and a maintenance officer who would serve as the pilot were going with me. We had caught a flight on a C-130 out of Phu Bai and gotten to Saigon late that afternoon.

Much of the next day had been spent at the facilities of the aircraft company on Tan Son Nhut airbase that had a contract to refurbish and upgrade several Chinooks for the Army. The folks that worked there had given us an extensive tour of their plant. It was obviously a quality facility that did some highly specialized work. Then came lots of paperwork and an extensive inspection of our "new" aircraft. Later that afternoon our maintenance officer had gone out with one of the company's test pilots for an acceptance flight.

We had planned to fly all the way back to Camp Eagle the next day, but an Army liaison officer asked us to fly a mission for an aviation unit at Vung Tau, on the coast southeast of Saigon. This unit flew the Mohawk (among other types of aircraft): a twin-engine, fixed wing Army reconnaissance airplane. There were three new Mohawks at Tan Son Nhut that the unit wanted airlifted to Vung Tau, and someone had come up with the idea that our new Chinook would be the perfect solution.

251

That "someone" apparently thought we could sling load them with ease. But I wasn't too sure—the thought of something going wrong and accidentally dropping a new multi-million-dollar aircraft into the jungle did not appeal to me in the least. I'd needed to clear it with my ops officer, so I put in a call to Camp Eagle. After he'd run it up our chain of command, the word had come down to fly the mission.

The next morning we were back at Tan Son Nhut airbase. After pre-flighting our aircraft, we had cranked up and flown a very short hop to where the Mohawks were located. As we'd hovered over the first one, I could see that there was a plank strapped to the upper surface of each wing. Those boards would serve as spoilers to interrupt the airflow over the wings and therefore prevent the possibility of the Mohawks "flying" on us (and causing potential damage or worse) as we slung them to Vung Tau. Another sight had caught my eye— there were several photographers there to capture the beginning of our mission. At the time, I didn't know if I should feel like a celebrity or if they were there to record an anticipated crash. As it was, our new aircraft with its heavier-lift engines performed the mission without difficulty. As we approached Vung Tau, I could see why it had a reputation as the resort assignment of Vietnam. The location was right on the coast with only a sand beach between the installation and the blue-green waters of the South China Sea. *How does someone get a posting like that?* I'd wondered. *Oh well, I'll be home in less than two months.*

Before the morning had passed we'd completed our three sorties and received a hearty thank you for it. After some lunch, we were on our way back north.

When we left Saigon, we had flown directly to the coast, then turned northeast. We'd made sure to stay far enough off shore so we could enjoy the scenery without taking any fire from bad guys. The view along the South Vietnam coast had been beautiful. The weather was clear, and the flight almost breathtaking. We'd gotten as far as Qui Nhon that evening where we decided to stay overnight before completing our flight to Camp Eagle.

The next day we'd known we were getting close to "home" when the familiar aerial view of Da Nang with China Beach, Marble Mountain, and the huge harbor, was already behind us. Another couple minutes and we'd come around the Hai Van Pass and into our AO. Not long after that we were setting down in the Locker Room, our mission to ferry a newly modified Chinook to Co. B. a success.

And today I had no flying at all. I'd sure enjoyed sleeping in. A leisurely breakfast and sipping some coffee sounded good before getting some things done — including letter writing.

*　　　*　　　*

6 June 70

Dear Donna,

It's an early, warm Saturday morning. I don't have to fly today so I'm going to try to get caught up on some letter writing, starting with you. It's already getting warm this early, and we usually hit 100 by noon. In the afternoon, the cumulo-nimbus clouds are [normally] towering majestically above the mountains. There are usually heavy, scattered thundershowers in the afternoon, which I make a point to fly around instead of through.

You know, I'm worried that I won't have much of a tan by the time I get home. For the past two months or more, I really haven't had a chance to flake out on the bunker because I've been too busy. And now it's almost too hot to catch some rays. Such are the troubles I have in a combat zone...

Let's see now. I guess you could say that I have all of 48 days left to go. I'm getting so short I can hardly live with myself anymore. Most of the new guys (remember, I'm the old-timer) regard me with almost awe. Every once in awhile I favor them with a few words of wisdom, but not too often.... Not only do I have 48 days left in country, I also have just 45 days left in company. We leave company three days prior to DEROS for out-processing at Phu Bai and Cam Ranh Bay (Cam Ranh Bay is where I get my Freedom Bird). And since we quit flying ten days prior to leaving company, I now have a maximum of 35 flying days remaining!

By the time this gets to you, you will probably have already gone through your graduation exercises.... Knowing how fond of flowers you are, I really wanted to send you some. However, the only flowers in the Camp Eagle area I could find were a couple blossoms [by an aircraft revetment]. They have [floral] wire services in Da Nang, but I haven't been there in some time. They don't even carry graduation cards in the PX here. I feel terrible about this. I guess this letter is the best I can do to say congratulations. I'll tell you what. I will take you out to dinner for your graduation, okay? Even if it is a little late...

[Regarding your question from your latest letter:] Do ducks have lips? Now that's an interesting question. I really think they do. I've been out hunting ducks in the ponds, lakes, and streams of S. Dak., and I know those ducks were making out in the early morning hours. What a mind I have...

Love, Dale

Chapter 38

…let justice roll on like a river…

Amos 5:24 (NIV)

Spring 1970

It was early afternoon, but I had to break off from humping loads and go to a meeting at Camp Eagle. My crew was more than pleased to have the rest of the day off.

Periodically we were involved with moving artillery batteries into new or previously abandoned firebases. That was especially true with the advent of the dry season a couple months ago. Generally, one of the more experienced ACs would serve as the assault commander for the mission. It was my turn to be commander for the next move.

I found my way to the underground ops bunker where the meeting was to take place. It didn't take too long to go through all the elements of the move: location, type and number of artillery pieces, number of security forces, number of battery personnel, initial complement of supplies, gunship escorts, and several other details. After we had estimated the number of sorties, established their sequence, determined the radio frequencies, and of course set the date and time the move would take place, the meeting was over.

As I exited the bunker and walked toward a gate, I lit a cigarette. Just then a guard by the gate gave me a salute. I hadn't noticed him before so was a little surprised, and my unthinking reaction was to give him a return salute, per military protocol. Unfortunately I had that just-lit cigarette in my mouth as I saluted — not good protocol. At the same time, I noticed out of the corner of my eye an officer standing about fifty feet away, watching. He motioned me over. *Oh, crap, a light (lieutenant) colonel. Just stand at attention, eyes straight ahead, no emotion on your face, and DON'T SAY A WORD.*

The officer's jaws were tight and his face unsmiling. He laid into me: "Mr. Petersen, you know you have no business saluting with a cigarette in your mouth. I know you've probably been flying ten- or twelve-hour days, day after day, week after week, getting shot at, worrying about your aircraft and crew, not getting enough sleep, exhausted."

Yeah, you got it about right so far.

"That's no excuse for what you just did. That young specialist is proud of his job and proud to give you a salute. And your response is to show him no respect by saluting with a cigarette in your mouth."

Yes, I'm depraved.

"Don't you ever let that happen again. Dismissed!"

"Thank you, sir," I lied as I saluted him, making sure my lit cigarette was in my left hand by my side.

As I walked back to Varsity, I didn't know whether to laugh or be angry. He was correct as to the letter of protocol "law." But I felt an injustice had been done to me because I hadn't gotten a chance to explain my extenuating circumstances. Then I chuckled to myself: *You'll never see him again anyway. Let that be a lesson, Petersen: quit smoking.* But I didn't.

That evening I kicked back at the Gork for another forgettable movie. As it was droning on, my mind wandered up to the flight line because I could also hear a Chinook somewhere up there running at flight RPM. I guessed it was a maintenance test ground run which often happened after some types of repair activity. Just then came the sound of thrashing, smashing, tearing metal. The sounds emanating from the flight line had changed decidedly—the engines were still turning but the rotors definitely were not. In a split second most of the Gork Theater emptied out as a herd of Varsity guys headed for the flight line on the run.

As I arrived, I saw a Chinook in an attitude I'd never before seen—it was lying on its side, almost on its top, sprawled across one of the walls of the revetment. The rotor blades were wildly askew, bent here, broken there. About that time, the engines wound down and stopped—someone had made his way inside to the cockpit and shut it down. That was a brave thing to do since leaking fuel could be smelled and seen around the aircraft. Both the maintenance officer and the flight engineer who'd been conducting the test run were out of the aircraft. They appeared to be okay although were both limping somewhat and showing signs of sore backs.

The maintenance officer wasn't completely sure what had happened, but from his description of the incident, it seemed that the aircraft had somehow become airborne and then rolled enough for the rotor blades to contact the ground and the helicopter to crash on its side.

Since it was dark, he hadn't seen it happening. One theory was that the brake on the thrust lever had malfunctioned, and the thrust lever had vibrated upward to put enough pitch in the blades to become airborne. That seemed pretty far out to me, but not beyond the realm of possibility. Although the rotor blades were all destroyed, most of the Chinook was amazingly intact with little noticeable damage. The last we saw of that aircraft, it was swinging gently underneath a CH-54 Flying Crane helicopter as it was being airlifted to a depot repair facility.

There was no way the movie that night could top the excitement we'd had on the flight line.

Chapter 39

*All his sons and daughters came to
comfort him,
but he refused to be comforted. "No,"
he said,
in mourning will I go down to the
grave to my son."
So his father wept for him.*

--Genesis 37:35 (NIV)

9 June 70

Dear Donna,

...[DEROS is] really starting to seem like a short time away. When I think that I've been here 320 days, [it] really seems like I've been gone a long time. But when I look back over it, it doesn't seem so long — the time has really gone fast. I'll know that I'm really short when they close out my flight records ten days before I leave this company. My only regret about leaving is that I cannot take my friends back to the world with me. I wish they wouldn't have to stay here any longer than me...

Last Saturday we had a big company cookout. (Every Saturday the officers have a barbecue, but this was the whole company....) [T]his was to celebrate our getting a superior rating on the annual Adjutant General's Inspection (AGI). Yup, they even give inspections in a combat zone. It's really stupid as far as I'm concerned, but what can we do? We can't fight the sacred institution of the Army. Well, anyway, we had good ol' potato salad, barbecue beans, lobster, and steaks. I had a little bit of everything (or should I say a lot of everything). I still like steak better than lobster. We had some good ol' golden suds to go with the food. Really hit the spot...War sure can be tough sometimes. After a weekend like that, I'm not sure if I want to leave here or not. HA!

What really made the weekend great, though, was that I got to go to chapel. It was [a] communion service which made it a double blessing for me. I really appreciate days like that, and I can't help but thank God for all He has done for me. It will be so great to be able to go to services regularly again...

About your question of it being harder to write the "shorter" I get: Yes, it does get increasingly difficult. Can't really explain it, but other guys say the same thing, so maybe it's natural...

Love, Dale

*   *   *

13 June 70

Dear Donna,

It's an early Sat. morning. I'm supposed to be flying now, but my aircraft is having some maintenance difficulties. I figured I'd whip out a few lines to you, and then get some extra sack time. Since it's Saturday, I really should have the day off to go to the beach or something. I gotta get <u>some</u> rays before I leave this place.

Speaking of leaving this place, I guess I could give you an update on the latest statistical data pertaining to leaving. Wait one while I count it up...okay, I've got it now. <u>41</u> days! (or, as we say it, 40 days and a wakeup)...

You asked if I felt the same way about Cambodia now. Well, that confuses me about as much as this whole war does. There's no disputing the fact that [U.S. forces] did uncover a lot of good stuff. But as we pull out, how long will it take Chuck to go back into his sanctuaries and replenish his supplies? And who knows just how many millions of tons of supplies were not uncovered? In other words, how really effective was that little venture? Did it really save the lives of thousands of U.S. troops, or were those few hundred troops who died in Cambodia sacrificed for no reason? I don't know the answers to these questions. I don't think anybody does. It may prove to have been the biggest life-saving and war-

shortening effort of this war. I just don't know. I am not a pacifist of any sort. I am just a confused person who has many questions about this. One thing I am not confused about, though, is that in the past year I have really found out how precious human life is. It is not something to shrug your shoulders about and say, "We have to figure on losing a few bodies. But we have replacements for them." A human life isn't something to be played with. And a lot of this war has turned into just that: playing with human lives. I guess every war has that to a certain extent. I guess that is why war is such a sub-human form of existence. What's really bad is that many wars are necessary...

Nope, I haven't seen any "clogs," but with that description, they sound kinda weird... Yup, I suppose things have changed quite a bit since I've been in the States. I think I'll wait until I've been home awhile before buying some clothes. I think I'll just put on my love beads, cut-offs, and sandals and cool it that way.

Hope that you are feeling better. I am praying for you. Take care of yourself now, and I'll see you soon.

Love, Dale

Chapter 40

*I am with you and will watch over you
wherever you go...*

--Genesis 28:15 (NIV)

16 June 1970

Another early wake-up. The ops clerk didn't need to tell me my missions. We'd been briefed last night on the one that would take up the better part of this day. It was to be a big, complicated artillery move into an old firebase just a couple miles west of the Ashau Valley. Today would be the closest we'd get to that old nemesis yet this year. I was glad I'd already completed my turn as an artillery assault commander a few days ago and wasn't in charge of this one.

I hadn't slept too well last night—my paranoia about getting wounded or killed with only a few weeks to go probably didn't help. I figured I'd better have an extra cup of coffee at breakfast.

After breakfast I grabbed my flight helmet, chicken plate, survival vest, map box, and other paraphernalia and headed for the flight line. As I approached my assigned aircraft, I could see the silhouettes of the flight engineer and crew chiefs on top of the Chinook against the brightening eastern sky as they went through their preflight inspection. I stopped a moment to take in the tranquil beauty of the scene. The reddish orange of the early morning was dissolving into a brighter, yellow tone as the sun pushed its way closer to the horizon. I wondered if I would miss the natural splendor of this place when I was home. Immediately, though, I chastised myself for such sentimentality: *Okay, Petersen, you are an idiot. You need to stay alive, get out of this place by 24 July, and never look back.*

After my pilot and I had gone through our preflight, we strapped in, summarily went through our checklist, and soon the turbines were whining and the rotor blades turning. As usual, I exercised my prerogative as the AC and made the first takeoff of the day. There was still something thrilling about pulling up on that thrust lever, bringing the front wheels off the ground, then leaping straight up into the air. I relished that feeling of power as the Chinook rose easily into the sky, then tipped the nose forward and rapidly increased airspeed.

In less than ten minutes we were at our pick-up point. Our helicopter had the second load of the move. Some Hueys would insert a security force, then the first Chinook would arrive with the advance troops of the artillery battery. Our initial load would be the first tube, a 105-mm artillery piece with a complement of ammo in a sling underneath the gun. The next five loads after ours would be the remainder of the artillery pieces which made up the battery. In this way the battery would be able to be employed with all six guns and fire several rounds if necessary after the first seven Chinook sorties. After the six tubes were in place, there would be several sorties with more pax (passengers), lots of ammo, water and fuel bladders, and a myriad of other items necessary for the battery to operate for an extended period.

As I was bringing the Chinook to a hover, I spotted my load — it was the one that had a guy standing on it with a donut for the hook in his hand. As I approached the load, I made sure that the barrel of the gun was oriented in the same direction as my Chinook. One of the first things we learned is never approach an artillery piece from the front because you'd probably end up with the tube puncturing the belly of your helicopter.

"Sir, got your load in sight," came the voice of the flight engineer over the intercom. "Forward twenty, down ten. ...You are over your load... load is hooked up... loader is free of gun. ...Slack is out of strap. Gun is off ground. Slack is out of ammo net. Ammo net is off ground. ...You are clear."

We reported in to the assault commander and were given clearance to depart for our objective. We would continue to monitor the assault radio frequency. Air Force F-4s were already prepping the area prior to the arrival of the security force. It didn't seem like more than a couple minutes that the Hueys with the security force were already on final approach into the firebase, escorted by Cobra gunships. The first word we heard from them was that they hadn't taken any fire. That was encouraging. When we were about five minutes out from our objective, the first Chinook was just setting down on the firebase with the initial cadre from the arty battery. It didn't take long for the pax to exit the aircraft and the Chinook was airborne—again without taking fire.

About that time our gunship escorts came alongside us since it was our turn next. My pilot contacted the pathfinder, and we were given clearance to come in with our load. Someone on the ground popped a purple smoke grenade to indicate where they wanted the load. As we began our descent into the firebase, the "snakes" on either side of us fired a few rockets and several bursts from their mini-guns along our flight path. As I got close to the firebase, I could see a G.I. holding his hands up to indicate where we were to drop our load.

About that time, the flight engineer took over: "Sir, got your drop zone in sight. Forward fifty, down twenty, left five. ...Okay, your ammo net is nearing the ground. Forward five. ...Okay, straight down. ...Ammo net is on the ground. Give me some slack. Okay, right five. ...Tube is clear of ammo net. Set down your load. ...Load is on the ground. Give me some slack. ...Okay, load is punched off. You are clear for departure."

I pulled up pitch and with the sling load no longer underneath us, the Chinook quickly gained altitude from its hover. We ascended rapidly, spiraling upward. I wanted to get as much distance between us and the ground as swiftly as possible. I breathed a sigh of relief as we had taken no fire, which we reported to the assault commander. Once we were high above the rugged mountains and jungle, I said to my pilot, "You got it."

When he responded, "I got it," I released the controls and could feel the tension drain from my body. My muscles relaxed, and I lit a cigarette. I could see the next five loads inbound, about two minutes apart, one already almost over the firebase. I looked down at the wild and foreboding terrain, glad I was where I was, high above it. Each sortie reported no fire. I imagined ol'

Chuck was keeping his head pretty low what with all the firepower we had going in there.

The move went smoothly and came off without a hitch. The battery was in action within a few minutes of the last tube being set in place. By midday all the scheduled loads had made it to the firebase. We flew the rest of the afternoon, mostly our typical missions of resupply to various firebases in our AO.

That evening, back at the Locker Room, I found out two pieces of good news: I didn't have night standby bird duty, and I had the next day off. It seemed like they were really cutting me some slack now. It didn't hurt that we had quite a few new aircraft commanders now, so there were more ways to share the workload. A movie and a long night of sleep sounded so good. Tomorrow I'd try to get some rays on top of the bunker. ...But I knew that by late morning it'd be too hot to be up there. *Ah, I'll worry about that tomorrow.*

Chapter 41

You will not fear the terror of
night,
nor the arrow that flies by day,

--Psalm 91:5 (NIV)

Dale H. Petersen

24 June 70

Dear Donna,

...I had finally been getting better at getting more letters written to you, and now I've relapsed again...To tell you the truth, though, you won't be getting too many more letters from the Far East, any way you look at it. Stop a moment and look at the date at the top of the page. This marks the end of eleven months here. Exactly one month from this very moment, I'll be waiting to board the Freedom Bird taking me home! I'm just too short for words. I'm so short I can almost hold my breath till DEROS. I get more nervous as the time gets shorter. I always try to stay within a short running distance of the bunker. Kinda stupid, huh? I'm glad I only have about 16 flying days left. Then I can just cool it till I leave.

Remember I had told you they were starting to cut me some slack and giving me a few days off? Well, for the past week or so, I've been flying just as much or more than I ever have. Two of our ACs (aircraft commander) are on R & R, and one AC went down to Saigon to pick up another new aircraft, so...the load falls back on us. The past two days have been the worst. The day before yesterday, I got up at 4 a.m., took off at 5:45 a.m., and got back in at 7:45 p.m. That's a long day anyway you look at it. You'd think they would pay overtime wages. The worst thing was that I was flying with a brand new guy who didn't know left from right, so I was busy pulling my hair out, trying to keep things squared away. When I finally got in, I was more or less like a zombie. Well, yesterday it was about the same thing. Didn't fly quite as long (got in by

6 p.m.). *I flopped in my bed about 7 p.m. and didn't wake up till 8 a.m. today. I was happy to find out I had the day off.*

A couple days ago a ground unit operating in the Khe Sanh area got hit bad by the gooks. We carried in a battalion of troops as a relief force near the area. Then we put in two batteries of artillery into two different firebases to support them. It was a busy, mixed-up day coming on such short notice. The last I heard was that the bad guys got caught with their pants down and got their tails kicked because of the quick reaction time.

Do you realize that I have gotten three letters from you in the past four days? WOW! How do I rate? Not only that, but I also got an envelope containing a questionable picture of two young ladies planting a lip lock on the governor [of Michigan]. That could [have] some implications on the ethics of public officials in their private lives...I think I've been reading too many newspapers. Anyway, that was really a cute picture. I had fun showing it around to all the guys...

What do I think about when I think of coming to Detroit? Well, mainly I think of happiness and having fun. I don't usually think of anything specific. Sometimes I think of Windsor [where we'd looked at the nighttime skyline of Detroit on our first date]...Tiger's Stadium (Yuk!), a quiet, relaxed evening in front of a TV, or an evening dinner with soft music...One picture I see in my mind most often though, is walking through the zoo with you, just cooling it [in] my cutoffs and sandals. That's the most recurring picture I have. I can't really explain it; I guess it just has an air of pure happiness and enjoyment. It'll be the greatest just being able to

*be in the companionship [of] and being able to talk to the person
who I know mostly through letters…*

…I'll be seeing you real soon.

Love muchly, Dale

*   *   *

27 June 70

Dear Donna,

*I just flew about four hours this morning and had some
maintenance problems, so it looks like I might get the rest of the
day off. That's quite all right. Gives me a chance to write you
a letter. I owe my parents a letter, too, so I can get that out of
the way today…*

*The night before last was largely a sleepless night. At
about midnight ol' Chuck started pouring mortars in here. We
were on red alert for a couple hours and finally went to bed at 2
a.m. At 3 a.m., I was again rudely interrupted, this time by
rockets. Fortunately, we had only one of our aircraft
damaged…I just hate rocket attacks. They're one of the most
frightening experiences I have to go through, I guess mainly
because they usually come at night.*

…Be seeing you soon; until then, take real good care.

Love, Dale

Chapter 42

*Wisdom, like an inheritance, is a good
thing
and benefits those who see the sun.*

--Ecclesiastes 7:11 (NIV)

Dale H. Petersen

Dear Donna,

Today is the last day of June, and already half of 1970 is past history. It seems such a short time ago that Bob Hope was here and that it was New Year's Eve, the [beginning] of a new decade. And now I have just 24 days left here, eleven flying days. Just three weeks from Friday I'll be stepping on the Freedom Bird, my tour in Vietnam having been completed. It hasn't been an easy year, but it's a year I will never forget. I guess I could say it's been a good learning experience. I have learned a lot about life, people, and things. I have also learned a lot about myself. Ever since I read the book Red Badge of Courage *in high school, I have wondered inside of me how I would react if I was ever under fire. Well, I have been under fire on occasion, and now I know. I guess in some ways I've become a man this past year; in other ways I think I'm still a boy. It's been a long year, sometimes filled with joys and happiness, sometimes filled with tears and sorrow. I still think quite often of [...] Big George and Little George, Vandy and Arnold; guys I've lived with, [flown] with, worked and played with, and now they are no more. Oh heck, I've gotta quit this or I'll have myself crying like a little baby. I don't really know why I've been telling you all this...I'm glad I can talk to you.*

I've got a day off again so I'll have a chance to do my laundry. Maybe I'll get my bodd out in the sun, too...

Got a letter from you which was really great, as always. So my dear ol' Dad told you, "I'm sure he'll stop here on the way to Georgia." That sounds like something he would say. He's always a big kidder. I got a kick out of reading it. No, I wasn't kidding about the beaches here. They are beautiful, and so is the water of the South China Sea. In peacetime, this could be a great resort nation, kinda like the Riviera along the Mediterranean. And they could also build some beautiful villas in the mountains. I don't think I'll ever want to come back here again, though. At least that's the way I feel now.

That's about it for now. Take care... and I'll see you real, real soon!

Love, Dale

Chapter 43

*...proclaim liberty throughout the land
to all its inhabitants...*

--Leviticus 25:10

4 July 1970

I slowly awakened from a deep sleep. It seemed to be fully light outside my hootch, and I could hear sounds of guys up and around. The familiar *whop-whop-whop!* of Huey rotor blades hitting the air were out there somewhere above Camp Eagle. With the hundreds of Hueys assigned to the 101st Airborne Division, and most of them located at Camp Eagle, I doubt there was a span of more than a few minutes throughout the entire year I spent in Vietnam that the sound of a Huey wasn't ringing in my ears. Maybe that's an exaggeration, but not by much. I could also hear an airborne Chinook, probably fresh off the ground from the Locker Room. Mike, the ops officer, had told me last night that I probably wouldn't be flying today, but he couldn't guarantee it. So far, it was looking like I had another day off. No complaints from me. Only six more possible days of flying. I hoped they'd be "milk run" missions (easy missions with no bad guy activity).

The Fourth of July. I wondered what my family would be doing today. When we'd lived in South Dakota, we'd almost always have a church potluck picnic at Platte Lake. I'd loved it, of course. Before going to the picnic, my brother Don and I would ride our bikes in the cool of the morning out to the edge of town where fireworks were sold along the highway. We needed to make sure we had an ample supply of firecrackers for the day. Besides, firecracker buying was just something you did on the Fourth, the informal first commandment for proper behavior on that most celebrative of the secular holidays. Midday would find us at the lake, gorging ourselves on the best dishes the church cooks had in their repertoire. My sincere regret each Fourth was that there was no way I could sample every dish. After eating, and after waiting the requisite half hour, it was into the lake and swimming for as long as I wanted or until we had to go home—whichever came first. Swimming wasn't the only activity on the calendar, however. We would also be treated to a pickup softball game played by some of the church men (unbelievably including Dad!). There was a certain incongruity in watching these men; even some of the church elders, with their normally somber demeanors, could be seen out there playing a game, smiling or even laughing. Watching them was like a guilty pleasure—probably because it was such a rare thing—so much so that I often gave up some swimming time to watch the game. And finally, going home at the end of the day never signaled the end of the festivities, because the day would be capped off by a brilliant fireworks display in Platte.

Now that we lived in Washington, the family would probably be going just a few miles north and east into British Columbia to Cultus Lake, and would largely repeat the South Dakota Fourth of July experience. If only I could be there now. But there were still a few more July days to elapse before I could go home.

We would be celebrating the Fourth in Varsity as well. A big company blowout was being planned later this afternoon with steaks on the grill, beer, and all the best of the picnic side dishes. No fireworks, though, unless Charlie lobs some rockets in here.

I thought about the Fourth and what it represented—a declaration of independence for our country. We had so many freedoms in our country. I knew that when I went home and got out of the Army, I could go to college, anywhere I wanted. I could get a job doing whatever I wanted to do, as long as I could get someone to hire me. I could live wherever I decided, I could believe and worship however I chose. Freedom of movement, freedom of activity, freedom of thought. And so much more. Kinda cool. Really cool. Would fighting this war or not fighting it change these freedoms in any material way? Probably not. But the harder question was: would fighting this war affect the freedoms of South Vietnam? If the North took over, I was pretty sure there would be quite a negative impact on the South. The problem was, I didn't see the South having all that much freedom right now. Probably kind of hard for that to happen when there'd been a war raging for the last several years. I sure didn't think I could call their current government or recent elections very democratic, at least in the way we understand it in the U.S. And were we really fighting this war effectively? Or were we just getting lots of American and Vietnamese kids killed only to have the NVA and VC wait us out and survive, and in that way win? I just didn't know. I wished God would somehow show us clearly what was right and wrong in this. All I really knew was that I wanted to be able to go home, safe and sound. That was probably selfish, but it was my overwhelming feeling at the moment.

I couldn't wait to get home. I was getting so excited — it would happen this month. It was almost all I could think about. I'd get so excited that my nerves would tighten up, and I'd get the shakes. It had been so long that I'd been gone. A year was an awfully long time.

I decided it was finally time to haul my body out of bed. It felt good just to let myself wake up slowly. I thought about practicing being lazy today so I'd be ready when my flying days in Vietnam were over.

Chapter 44

God is our refuge and strength,
a very present help in trouble.

--Psalm 46:1 (KJV)

6 July 1970

We'd been working most of the day up in the neighborhood of the "Z." There continued to be a lot of activity in that part of our AO. As happened every once in awhile, I was feeling grateful that I wasn't a grunt, that I was flying instead. The thought of having to pound through that thick jungle this close to my DEROS was just too awful to contemplate. I hoped all this ammo we'd been hauling into those mountain firebases was doing those guys some good.

The thunderheads had been building over the past several hours. Those magnificent, fearsome-looking masses of clouds were rising thousands of feet into the sky. The underside of those formations began to take on ominous, dark hues. Unfortunately, we still had at least a couple hours' worth of sorties, and given the amount of bad guy activity, this was not the time to short-change the firebases, if at all possible.

As the afternoon wore on, the winds increased and the turbulence over the mountains made me think of what it might be like if I were to take a turn in a spinning clothes dryer. Nonetheless we were able to get into most of the firebases with all the assigned loads. A couple times it was necessary to delay an approach because a firebase was in the clouds and weather, but we were able to finally get almost everything delivered.

After our last load was dropped off, I felt a wave of relief as we exited the mountainous zone and found ourselves over the relatively smooth air of the coastal plain. What I hadn't counted on was the dark mass stretched across the southern sky and our route home. About that time Phil radioed Freddie and me over our company frequency. The three of us had been working the northern mission most of the day. We talked over the weather situation and decided it was best to stay over Highway 1 and get down on the deck before we got into the rain. In case it got too bad, we could set down at Camp Evans or LZ Sally, both of which were very close to the highway. I could see Phil in front of me so I decided to close up with him. Freddie had just finished his last load and was a ways behind us.

It wasn't long before it was raining in earnest. We went down to about fifty feet AGL. The rain was pounding on our aircraft—the windshield wipers could barely keep up with it. We both dropped down a little lower over the highway to keep a watery visual contact with the ground. Although it was still supposed to be daylight, it seemed more like nighttime. The sky had an eerie, dark-yellowish glow. Highway 1 was living up to its nickname again: "Street Without Joy." Actually, the water on the pavement made the highway stand out in the gathering gloom. Every so often the buff color of grass huts in small farming villages would pass beneath us, an affirmation that we had enough—just enough—visibility. We passed LZ Sally, the last best place to set down before Camp Eagle. Next we skirted Hue, which meant it was just a few more minutes to Camp Eagle. We got tower clearance for a low-level approach to the

Locker Room, and familiar landmarks pointed us home. An empty revetment in Varsity Valley came invitingly into view. I brought the aircraft to a hover in the valley, then slowly nursed it into the revetment and set it down. It was only then that I became aware of the excessive tension in my body, how sore my back, neck and head were.

After we shut down Phil and I talked about the wild ride home. We hadn't heard from Freddie for awhile and were getting concerned. It had turned completely dark and was still raining. Then we heard the rumbling of a Chinook approaching our area. In a moment the aircraft was overhead—coming in low, position lights and rotating beacon on, searchlight showing the way ahead.

"There he is," I said, breathing more easily. But the next moment, the Chinook suddenly went black as all its lights went out.

"Oh, no…"

I tensed, waiting for a crash or something even more unexpected. I could still hear the whine and pounding of engines and rotor blades. In another instant, all the lights flashed on again.

"Oh, man, what happened?"

"I thought he was dead."

It wasn't long before we saw Freddie in the flesh, with a big grin on his face. "What the heck happened?" I asked.

"We must have had an electrical failure. I just reached up and recycled the generator switch and the lights came back on."

I just shook my head. "Man, I don't think I would have ever thought of that."

Freddie tried to remain nonchalant, but his smile was looking more like a grimace. "That was a bit too scary for me."

My whole body was sore, which made the chow taste extra good that night. It had been a long time since I had felt so much relief at being back on the ground.

I felt wiped out, so was in my rack early and sleeping a deep sleep about the time my head hit the pillow.

KAWUMP! "Incoming!"

Before I'd even woken up I was on the floor, pulling my mattress over me. As my brain cleared, I could hear 122s impacting, but I couldn't tell where. Then I heard another explosion close by and an accompanying cacophony of ripping wood and metal. My breath was shallow and my body shaking. *Oh God, I don't need this. Please!*

Then I was on my feet, running to the bunker. We soon found out that a rocket had landed about ten feet from the flight line end of the officer's living area. No one was hurt, but there was damage to the club, a hootch at the end of one row, and a metal storage container.

After the late night interruption of over an hour, I was in my bed again. I felt so exhausted but couldn't get to sleep for awhile. I almost willed myself to stay awake, perhaps thinking that if I didn't go to sleep we wouldn't get rocketed again. Finally my body succumbed and a deep slumber enveloped me.

The next morning we found out what a close call there had been from the rocket attack. There was a shrapnel hole about one inch in diameter in the wall of the hootch closest to the rocket impact. The hole was just a couple inches above the bed of one of the guys, almost exactly where his head would have been had he not gotten out of bed. That was much too close.

Chapter 45

...darkness was upon the face of the deep.

--Genesis 1:2 (KJV)

8 July 1970

It had been a full day of flying, but now it was late afternoon, the missions were complete, and I had already shut down in the Locker Room. That left just two more possible days of flying. The end was so close I could almost taste it. Could it, would it really, come to an end?

I had a pleasant evening ahead of me—a cold brew awaited me in my room, then some chow. I had heard the movie that night was going to be "Butch Cassidy and the Sundance Kid," a movie I'd been hoping to see for quite some time. It had finally made it to Northern I Corps.

I went into ops to drop off my map case. On the way out the door, Mike said, "Hey, Pete, I gotta have you take the night standby bird tonight."

Ugghh! Forget the brew. Bye, bye relaxing evening.

"Hopefully you won't need to launch. Plus, this is the last time you'll ever have night standby."

My shoulders sagged and I sighed. "Okay. I'll go preflight my aircraft and then get some chow."

"You gonna watch 'Butch Cassidy' tonight?"

"Yeah, I'll be there. After that I'll probably just turn in."

"Okay, thanks Pete."

The food was okay that evening but not quite as satisfying as I had been anticipating. I figured I was feeling a little sorry for myself. After supper I meandered over to the club and shot the breeze for awhile with the guys before we emptied out the place for the evening's main attraction at Gork Theater. We weren't even a half-hour into the movie yet when my eye caught Mike heading my way: "We gotta launch the standby bird! Now!"

All my crew members were at the movie that night, so I told them: "Get to the aircraft and get ready to go. I'll be there in a minute, as soon as I get our mission info."

I followed Mike to ops to obtain my map case and get briefed on the mission.

"Okay, Pete, we've got a tactical emergency. A Huey was shot down west of Quang Tri but it's intact."

Crap, way up by the "Z" again.

"We need to get it out of there ASAP," he continued, "because it has some secret or top secret equipment on board. Could be something like a 'people sniffer' but I'm only guessing. They have some ground security there, and they're getting the Huey rigged with a sling right now. Once you get it picked up, it needs to go to Quang Tri. Here are the contacts on scene and also at Quang Tri. And here are the coordinates."

We got the map out and pinpointed the downed aircraft's location. It was in the transition zone between coastal plains and mountains, just a few miles south of the "Z." I circled the location, then folded the map up as small as I could and clipped it onto my thigh map holder which I would attach to my leg once I was in the cockpit.

When I got to our aircraft the flight engineer was already standing at the rear ready for engine start. Both door gunners and the pilot were in their seats. My pilot was a new guy, so I planned to do just about everything and have him sit on his hands. I think this was partly to try to decrease the odds of something bad happening so close to my going home. In other words, it was because of my paranoia. I quickly got the P started, then the two main engines. In a moment we were at flight RPM, and all instruments and caution lights said we were a go. After getting takeoff clearance, I lifted the Chinook into the inky blackness of the night.

As we headed northwest, I briefed the crew on our mission. Soon the lights of Hue appeared before us as Camp Eagle faded to the rear. Past Hue it seemed very dark, although I could make out a horizon. I turned off our position lights and our lower rotating beacon. I left on the upper rotating beacon so any other aircraft could see us, but hopefully no one on the ground could. After we passed by LZ Sally, we could see tracer rounds going back and forth on the ground. Apparently there was a firefight in progress, probably between U.S. troops and the VC or NVA. Long streams of red and green tracer rounds located the arc of small arms fire between the two groups of combatants. Red and green dots winked below us, like long strings of Christmas lights blinking off and on across city streets and village neighborhoods.

When the lights of Quang Tri came into view, I gave the frequency of our on-scene contact to my pilot and had him dial it in on our FM radio. I turned a little more to the west, bringing us away from Highway 1 and

Quang Tri and heading in the direction of our rendezvous with the downed Huey. About the same time the pilot extinguished our upper rotating beacon as I had instructed him. Anyone on the ground could surely hear us, but at least no one could see us now. Soon I reached down and turned my radio transmit dial to FM, then attempted to make contact with our friends on the ground.

"Roger, Varsity, I have you Lima Charlie [loud and clear]," came the response from our ground contact.

"Roger. Do you have a strobe light?"

"Roger that."

"Go ahead and activate it."

In just a few seconds I saw a rapidly blinking white light in front of us. I couldn't tell how far away it was because estimating distances at night, especially when a tiny light is all you could see, was very difficult for me. I guessed we were one or two miles away yet. "Got your strobe."

"Roger, Varsity, and we can hear you now."

"Okay, we'll be there shortly."

I would take it real easy on our descent. I had no ground references other than the horizon, and I wanted above all to maintain control of the aircraft. Since we didn't know the bad guy situation on the ground, the searchlight would stay off as long as possible. Once that searchlight was switched on, there would be a "blast" of light which could be seen for miles if the Chinook was too high above the ground.

I slowly felt my way down through the darkness, constantly referring to my airspeed indicator, attitude indicator, altimeter, and vertical velocity indicator. The strobe light was beginning to look closer and closer. I wanted to turn on the searchlight, but waited a little longer. I eased my already slow descent and airspeed. Somehow in the darkness I could tell we were nearing the ground and the strobe seemed quite close. We couldn't wait any longer, so I found the light switch on my thrust lever and turned it on. At the same time my left thumb found the searchlight control switch and pressed it forward to extend it from its normal retracted position. Suddenly, everything in front of us was bathed in light. The ground appeared to be less than one hundred feet below us. A Huey came into view, then another. I could see G.I.s moving around the lit area.

Then, thankfully, came the voice of the flight engineer over the intercom: "Sir, I got our load in sight. It's at our two o'clock."

Since I was at a hover, I did a right pedal turn and saw a Huey with a G.I. standing on it and holding a donut at the end of a sling. I slowly moved the Chinook forward.

"Forward fifty, down twenty."

As I passed over the Huey, I lost my stationary ground references and was looking instead at tall grasses, waving crazily back and forth due to our powerful rotor wash. The constant motion of the grass was making it difficult to know when our forward movement had stopped.

"Sir, you overshot the load. Back ten. ...Hold. ...You're drifting backward. Forward five, down two. ...Hold, hold. ...You are drifting forward. We overshot again. Back five, don't go any lower. ...We're drifting back again and coming up. Forward five, down five. ...We drifted past the load again."

With nothing but waving grass as a reference, I simply couldn't judge the movement of the aircraft with enough subtlety to keep from drifting. "Chief, see if you can get a guy to stand in front of my chin bubble," I said.

"Will do, sir." Then, a few seconds later, I heard him follow up: "Okay, I think they got the message."

A couple seconds after that, there he was. Looking down through my chin bubble I saw a G.I., standing like the Rock of Gibraltar amid the waving torrents of grass. Now I had my stationary ground reference.

"Got him. Let's get this sucker hooked up."

"Okay, forward five, down three. ...Our load is hooked up. ...Man is clear of load. Bring it up. ...Slack is out of sling. Load is coming off the ground."

My pilot was keeping the rotor RPM in the green with his beep switch. I nosed the Chinook forward, felt us go through translational lift, pulled in more power, and we were once again climbing into pitch blackness. I switched off my searchlight to make us invisible once again. I felt temporarily blinded after the light went off, but I stayed on my instruments through our climb.

"Thanks much, Varsity. There are a lot of guys eager to get out of here."

"My thanks to the guy who stood in front of me and helped me get our load hooked up."

As we gained altitude the lights of Quang Tri appeared on the horizon. It was a beautiful sight, and we reached it in a relatively short flight. I had my pilot radio our contact. During our approach we turned on our top rotating beacon again. We'd been given the location on the flight line at Quang Tri where we'd drop off our load, and on short final approach I saw someone directing us to the drop point.

"Sir, I have the drop zone in sight. Forward twenty-five. ...Okay, that's good. Bring it straight down. ...Load is on the ground. Give me some slack. ...Load is released. You are clear to depart."

Shortly we had tower clearance and were climbing once again into the night sky. I was filled with both relief and satisfaction at the completion of our mission. I could feel my body relax. As we passed by Camp Evans and headed toward LZ Sally, there were no more tracer rounds reaching out for targets on the ground. The blackness of the ground gave an aura of peacefulness once again. I hoped no G.I. had gotten hurt. I wondered if there was someone in that unit who was nearing his DEROS, who had just completed his last mission and would be going back to the rear tomorrow. If so, I suspected he felt just like I did. For me, just two more possible days of flying.

Beyond LZ Sally, the lights of Hue illuminated the southeastern sky. It was one of those aerial views that simply couldn't be matched.

Okay, Petersen, I said to myself, *don't get sentimental on me. I'm going home in a couple weeks and I don't ever want to come back here.* Once past Hue the lights of Camp Eagle came into view; this would probably be my last night approach into the Locker Room. Soon I was hovering into a revetment. I slowly descended until my back wheels touched ground, then brought the nose down till the front wheels made contact. I fleetingly thought about what an ordinary landing it was, a simple repetition of something I'd done hundreds of times in the past year.

After shutdown and necessary paperwork, I sought out Mike to brief him on our mission.

"Sorry, but 'Butch Cassidy' is long over. You want us to set up a projector in the club so you can see it now?" he asked.

"Nah, don't worry about it. I'm sure I'll get a chance to see it in the States," I said with a shrug. "I think I'll just kick back and relax for awhile."

"Go ahead and have a beer or two. I got another bird and crew on standby in case we get another mission."

"Sounds good," I said on my way out the door.

"Hey, Pete, good job. Oh, by the way, I've got some good news for you…"

Chapter 46

Come to me,
all you who are weary and burdened,
and I will give you rest.

--Matthew 11:28 (NIV)

I woke up slowly after a very deep, long, satisfying night of sleep. Once I was fully awake, I knew I was starving so decided not to waste any time getting to a big breakfast ASAP.

On my way back from the mess hall, in addition to being contented with a full stomach, I was still giddy about last night. I couldn't wait to get letters written to Donna and my parents, and get them in the mail today. As soon as I got back to my hootch, I grabbed some paper and a pen and began writing:

9 July 70

Dear Donna,

I'm finished! It's all over with! I can hardly believe it! Never again will I have to strap into the cockpit of a CH-47 Chinook in Vietnam! I'm just beside myself with happiness and excitement! I flew my last mission in Vietnam last night. I was supposed to fly tomorrow, but the operations officer told me last night after I came in that he was going to close out my flight records and that I could turn in my flight gear today. I wasn't about to argue with him at all. I just can hardly believe it!

And now I have spent 350 days or 50 weeks in Vietnam. It's all so unbelievable to me. After everything that's happened, after a year has almost past, I get to go home. Going home now seems like a tangible reality, not just a dream. I can almost taste it. (Does it sound like I'm excited?) It's going to be pure bliss when that Freedom Bird surges off the runway at Cam Ranh Bay and wings its way east over the Pacific.

299

Now all I have to do is try to relax and unwind. My nerves have really been on edge the past couple weeks. My last mission last night was no "milk run" either...

...Take care, and it won't be long at all anymore!

Much love,
Dale

*   *   *

14 July 70

Dear Donna,

It's 9 a.m., and I just got up and took a shower. That's the way I've been doing it the past few days: sleep until I get all slept out, take a shower, then just kinda lounge around till lunch time. Some life, huh? I've been getting some sun, too. It's real hot out, but the winds have been quite strong lately, so they keep the bodd reasonably cool. I just may have a little tan yet. Some guys tan real fast, but my light complexion takes longer. Oh well, I'm no marshmallow anymore. I'm going to have to get my tail in gear shortly, though, and start getting my things packed. I've got all my inoculations (ouch!) now, so I'm all set there.

Can you believe that I'll be in the States in ten days? I still can't believe it. I'll be leaving Varsity for good exactly one week from today. No tears shed here. My only regret is that I'll have to leave my friends here. I won't believe that I'm actually going home until that silver bird lifts off the runway at Cam Ranh Bay.

And now I'm in the doghouse again. First it was graduation, and now it's your birthday. I thought I'd be getting to Da Nang in the past few days, but such is not the case. I went up to the PX to get you at least a nice card, but their selection consisted of old Father's Day cards and Get Well cards. I know, I know, excuses, excuses. Well, I won't be in Vietnam much longer. I understand that consumer products in the world for this sort of thing are a little more plentiful. Anyway...[a] belated Happy Birthday to you. 18 years old now, huh? That's great! Now I can't be accused of "robbing the cradle" anymore...Well, 18 is a little different than 16...

I'm going to run now to the PX and see if they have suitcases. See you real, real soon now, and please take care of that pretty little head of yours.

Much love, Dale

Chapter 47

A time to weep and a time to laugh,
a time to mourn and a time to dance…

--Ecclesiastes 3:4 (NIV)

21 July 1970

I woke up with a start. A quick glance at the clock told me there were a few minutes to spare. Hey, I was wrong! I'd been sure we would get rocketed last night. And it hadn't happened! I was in one piece and I'd just spent my last night at Camp Eagle! Could it really be true? It had to be—I was really awake, and it was light outside.

I replayed the going away celebration last night that had been held for Dave, Phil, and me. We'd come over on the same flight a year ago, and we would be on the same Freedom Bird together in a couple days. The celebration was quite informal. We'd each gotten Varsity plaques, and the CO had said some nice things about each of us. I'd smiled inwardly as he poured it on a little thick. He was brand new, and he hardly knew us. We'd each gotten a turn to speak. I couldn't recall everything I'd said, but I did remember my concluding comments: "... always remember Les, Oscar, Big George, Little George, Vandy, Arnold and the other crew members we lost. And watch your altitude. I want you guys to come home too. I'm not going to miss this place, but I will miss you guys."

I looked at the clock again. I wanted to take a shower and get something to eat before we left, so I needed to get up now. "Hey, Phil, time to get up. It's finally our day."

"Ummh, uh."

"Phil, you gotta get up now."

303

"Uh, yeah, just a minute."

When I came back from the shower, Phil was still out. I dressed, and on my way out the door to the chow hall, I again said, "Phil, get up. You don't want to miss our ride to Phu Bai."

"Uh, yeah, I'll be there."

I enjoyed my last meal at Varsity, but still no Phil. Several of the guys wished me well. One had said previously he'd drop us off at Phu Bai on his way out for the day's missions. Phu Bai was the out-processing center for the 101st. Out-processing would take a couple hours or so, but we weren't scheduled to leave for Cam Ranh Bay until tomorrow. Typical Army hurry up and wait. Man, I wanted to get out of northern I Corps today in the worst way, but I realized it probably wouldn't happen. Oh well, at least we would be on our way.

When I got back to the hootch, Phil was still in bed, sleeping.

"Phil, you have *got* to get up! We leave in ten minutes!"

This time he jumped out of bed.

I grabbed my suitcase and started out the door. "I'm not waiting on you. I'm not going to miss this flight."

"I'll be there."

One more time I walked out to the flight line. I could see that Dave was already by the aircraft.

"Where's Lanza?" he asked as I approached.

"I tried to wake him several times. He just now got out of bed."

"The heck with him. We'll leave him."

As the Chinook's APU started, we went into the cargo compartment to take a seat. I looked back, and there came Phil, a bit disheveled, hauling his duffle bag.

"Man, you about missed it."

"I said I'd be there."

"Lanza, you're dang lucky. We were going to leave you, no crap," said Dave, a smile on his face.

In a couple minutes we were airborne for the five-minute hop east over the high hill to Phu Bai. When we touched down, all three of us went up and shook the hands of the guys in the cockpit, then stepped out onto the tarmac. In a moment the Varsity Chinook was airborne, for them just another day of missions in the AO. For us, a new day was dawning, a huge milestone in our lives—we were beginning our journey home.

We walked over to the processing center. Over the door was a sign that read: "All the way to the USA." The names of the fifty states were listed on either side of the door. Inside we found the typical Army paperwork mill: fill out this form and that form, check over this record and that record, make sure financial documentation was up to date and correct, and a myriad of other things. I didn't mind at all. I'd been waiting for this moment for almost a year, and I was going to savor it, even the paperwork. At the end of the process we found out we were scheduled for a C-130 flight to Cam Ranh Bay tomorrow.

"But there's a C-130 leaving in a couple hours, and you can stand by for that."

Ah, a ray of hope!

When we got to the terminal, that ray of hope dimmed a bit. The place was jammed with G.I.s waiting to leave Phu Bai. We checked in at the passenger counter and then sat down for another wait. At the out-processing center we'd run into a couple of Huey drivers with whom we were acquainted and who had been on the same flight with us from the States a year ago. The time passed quickly as we got reacquainted and traded war stories. The C-130 arrived, and after unloading passengers and cargo, began loading for the flight to Cam Ranh Bay. We didn't hold out much hope for getting a seat. But when the last five seats were filled, the names called were Magers, Lanza, Petersen, and our two Huey pilot friends. I couldn't believe it! It seemed almost too good to be true. We'd be in Cam Ranh Bay early in the afternoon! And that meant we'd be leaving Vietnam earlier than anticipated because no one got scheduled for a specific Freedom Bird until he had checked in at the out-processing center in Cam Ranh Bay, essentially a first come, first served situation.

I was feeling sky high as we lifted off the runway at Phu Bai, but I soon settled back in my canvas seat. I was going to read awhile, but the C-130 was noisy and cramped, so my mind started wandering. I was so excited to be leaving northern I Corps, but the thrill was tempered as I began to reminisce and my reflections settled on my twelve fellow Varsity members who would never sense the exhilaration I was experiencing, who left Vietnam only in body bags. Why did I get to go home in one piece? Was I more deserving than them? Were they less deserving than me? I had hit Vandy, I had been impatient and unkind to Phil Arnold, and for that I got to go home and they didn't? It didn't make any sense. I didn't know why it was the way it was.

Had I done my job? Had I done it the way I was supposed to? Had I supported my compatriots the way I should have? Had I been inhibited from doing what I needed to do by the fear I often felt? Had I been honorable? I thought I'd done my job most of the time, but I didn't know for sure. Should I hold my head up? I just didn't know. And now I get to go home.

Before I knew it, I could tell the C-130 was on final approach. I sat up and took in my surroundings again. Some guys looked reflective, but it was hard not to see happiness in most faces. I decided to try to celebrate this final chapter in Vietnam, a time that I was quite sure would never again be duplicated in my life, this strange juxtaposition of exquisite joy and intense sadness.

Chapter 48

They will celebrate your abundant goodness…

--Psalm 145:7 (NIV)

21 July 1970

Buses met us on the tarmac and brought us to the Cam Ranh Bay out-processing center. More lines, more waiting, more paperwork. But I was smiling. I was starting to believe that this was really happening, that I would actually be going home and soon. It turned out to be not too long before our presence was duly registered and we were free to kill some time. Before we headed for the O Club, we noted where the flight manifests were posted and where hopefully very soon our names would be listed on a flight to the world.

There was a lot of laughing and joking and making of plans for when we hit the States. I entered into the conversation but was distracted by thoughts of the flight manifests. Every few minutes I'd get up and leave the club and walk over to the building where manifests and schedules were available for viewing. New ones went up and old ones came down almost hourly, signifying newly scheduled departures and Freedom Birds already winging eastbound. Every so often the public address system would sound off in the compound, calling the next flight and advising passengers when and where to report: "Your attention please, flight number Alpha 5 Lima 3 to Travis Air Force Base will be departing in two hours at 1700. All passengers must be at the departure building in three zero minutes, at 1530. I say again, flight Alpha 5 Lima 3 to Travis departs at 1700 and passengers must be at the departure building at 1530."

"Pete, our flight isn't gonna leave any sooner just because you're the first one to know our number and take-off time," Dave said as I sat down in the club after one of my absences. "You got ants in your pants or something?"

"Yeah, okay. It's better than sitting around here. Do you guys realize some folks have left here less than twenty-four hours after arriving?"

"I bet we don't get out of here till the twenty-third."

"We'll see. Besides, even the twenty-third would be a day before we're supposed to be out of here."

After that, the conversation turned desultory again. I actually enjoyed shooting the breeze over a golden brew. But my mind kept wandering over to the flight manifest building, and my body soon followed. It was late afternoon as I walked into the now very familiar building for the umpteenth time. I scanned the newly posted manifests. Then I froze. I felt a tickle in my stomach and some sweat on my back. Right there in front of me it read: Petersen, Dale H. I again glanced over the list and saw Lanza and Magers as well. We had a flight number—Golf 2 Tango 4. I didn't know what those letters and numbers signified, but I didn't care because that was my ticket home. And our flight was going to Mc Chord Air Force Base in Washington! I'd be practically home! No long connecting flights home for me after we made it to the good ol' USA. I checked the easel which held the scheduling board and there it was,

G2T4 departing 0600 tomorrow, 22 July. We'd be here less than twenty-four hours. We'd be going home a full two days early!

I hustled back to the club, then calmly sauntered over to the table. "Well folks, there's news."

"So what is it?"

"What's it worth to you?"

"Knock that crap off and just tell us!"

"Well, okay, flight G2T4 departs for Mc Chord at six tomorrow morning, and we'll all be on it."

"All right!"

"Good stuff!"

"Pete, you live there—how far to the Seattle airport?"

"Probably no more than thirty miles."

After much excited discussion and everyone exploring possible plans for their final leg home in several different ways, we went over to the chow hall for some supper. Later we found bunks in the temporary barracks, took showers, and tried to get some sleep. Before I got in my bunk, though, I took one more walk over to the flight manifest building. Yes, our flight was still on the board for departure at 0600. There were already a few new flights with departures after us. This was an around-the-clock operation, cycling through each day, bringing replacements to Vietnam, then loading up the same airplanes with veteran G.I.s, transforming the aircraft into Freedom Birds. I had waited for this for a year, and it was finally happening.

Sleep did not come easily. It seemed that every time I drifted off, another announcement for another flight departure would come over the PA system. That would be followed by a few guys here and there getting out of bed, rustling around, and departing the barracks. Later that night I got into a deeper sleep.

Then I was awakened again to another announcement, but this time I sat up. *Wait a minute*, I said to myself. *I know the flight they just called was scheduled after ours.* I checked my watch and I panicked. It was almost 0600! I looked and saw that Dave and Phil were still sleeping in the bunks next to me.

"Hey, Dave," I whispered, "they skipped our flight and it's almost 0600."

Dave sighed and turned over. "A couple hours ago when they announced another flight, they also said ours was delayed."

"Delayed! What the heck? Why?"

"Didn't say. Go back to bed."

Instead I pulled on my fatigues and boots and made a beeline for the manifest building. There it was on the scheduling board. Flight G2T4. In place of "0600" was the word "delayed." I walked over to the counter and asked someone, "So, what's with G2T4?"

"They're having to do some maintenance on the airplane in Anchorage. It ran into something on the ground."

"Great. How long is that supposed to take?"

"Don't know. But the flight hasn't been cancelled yet."

"So why weren't we put on the next flight?"

"It doesn't work that way. Once you've been manifested, you keep that flight even if it's delayed. If it ultimately gets cancelled, then you'll be manifested on the next available flight. But we don't bump other folks off flights on which they're already manifested."

Oh, man, this was the height of injustice. It just plain wasn't fair. There's no way someone who arrived in Cam Ranh Bay after I did should get home before me.

I meandered back to the barracks. Phil was awake so I told him what I'd found out. He rolled over and went back to sleep. I tried to do the same, but there was no going to sleep now. I was very frustrated by then but tried to tell myself the worst that could happen would be going home on my original DEROS. I didn't find much comfort in that at the moment.

What happened after that was just about the longest day of my life. Over to the chow hall for breakfast ... hung around here and there, mostly at the club ... read for awhile but got tired of that ... tried a catnap but that didn't work ... lunch ... more of the same hanging around ... countless trips to check on the scheduling board ... countless guys leaving Cam Ranh Bay heading east over the Pacific (of course, they had arrived here after us) ... and then more of the same.

Late that afternoon I got a surprise: there on the scheduling board, flight G2T4 had a departure time:

2330, and that was tonight, not tomorrow. I walked up to the counter. "Is that departure time for G2T4 pretty firm?"

"Should be. It's airborne heading our way."

We might just get out of here on the twenty-second after all! It took about a split second and I was re-energized and excited again. I hustled over to the club and gave the guys the good news. We all seemed to relax again. Joking and laughing came easily once more. We started planning our leave time while we were home, although we'd all need a year instead of a month to fit in everything. We decided to get some supper since it would probably be awhile before we saw food again.

Finally there was the announcement we'd been waiting an eternity for, but in truth more like seventeen or eighteen hours: "Your attention please, flight number Golf 2 Tango 4 to Mc Chord Air Force Base will be departing in two hours at 2330. All passengers must be at the departure building in three zero minutes, at 2200 hours. I say again, flight Golf 2 Tango 4 to Mc Chord departs at 2330 and all passengers must be at the departure building at 2200."

The departure building was a picture of friendly chaos when we arrived. After going through our processing, we got a final speech: "Gentlemen, if you will look to my left, you will see several booths with curtains. You will each have to pass through one of those booths. Those booths are called amnesty booths. If you had any intentions of smuggling any drugs back to the

States, I strongly recommend you rethink that. When you get in that booth, you will have one last chance to get rid of those drugs without any sanctions against you. There is a slot in the booth to deposit your contraband. Once you open that curtain on the other side of the amnesty booth, there is no more amnesty. As you can see, on the other side of the booths are MPs with drug-sniffing dogs. I assure you, gentlemen, if you still have any drugs on your person, they will find you out. And if you are found with drugs, you will be court-martialed, and you will go to jail. So think very carefully before you complete your transit of the amnesty booths. Okay, you may now proceed through the booths. Once through the booths, exit the doors in front of you where there are buses to take you to your USA-bound flight. Thank you, and have a safe flight home."

Most people sailed through the amnesty booths, but I noticed in a couple instances some time elapsed before a person exited. I couldn't wait to get through my booth and get on a bus. Soon we were en route, and I noticed my watch showed that it was after 11 p.m. when we pulled onto the tarmac. And then, there it was, our Freedom Bird! A chill went through my body as I stared at the Seaboard World charter DC-8. That thing of beauty was going to take me home.

Entering the door of the airliner brought me into a whole new world, one that was vaguely familiar somewhere in my brain, but something I had not experienced for a long time. Greeting me and everyone

315

else was a smile and a welcoming voice from home. The cool, air-conditioned cabin seemed tingly and pleasant. Before us spread comfortable, clean seats, not a hint of grease or dirt. It didn't take long for everyone to get settled. For some reason my thoughts wandered to rockets and mortars. We were almost free of their threat, but not quite. There was an old story, told many times, that just as a Freedom Bird was getting ready for take-off, mortars started hitting the airfield. Everyone on that airplane yelled and hollered, "Go, go, don't even think about not going!" The pilot complied. I had serious doubts; it definitely had the ring of a legend. But I also think it accurately portrayed the sentiment of everyone on board our flight.

The engines started whining, and we were taxiing by 11:30 p.m. In short order we were at the end of the runway, and just like that, the pilot hit full throttle and the jet was hurtling down the runway. I held my breath, the nose came up, and we were soaring into the night sky. A tremendous cheer went up in the cabin. I thought, *Get altitude quick! Get over the South China Sea now!* We rose higher and higher. We banked right and the sea was below us. A couple minutes later, the pilot's voice came over the intercom: "I'm sorry to have to report that we've just left the territorial waters of Vietnam." Another deafening roar filled the DC-8. We were truly on the way. No more worries about bad guys directing fire at us. It was happening, and it was real.

It didn't take long before we had dinner on our tray tables. After a satisfying meal, I tried to go to sleep, but there was no chance of that happening any time soon. In just a few hours dawn was breaking as we landed at Yokota Airbase outside Tokyo for a refueling stop. I got off the plane to stretch and browse a little in the terminal BX, but mainly I just wanted to get going.

Within an hour we were airborne again for the long stretch of our flight, but this was our last leg to Mc Chord and the States. This time I laid back and was fast asleep in no time. The next roughly nine hours found me eating yet another meal, reading, watching a movie, sleeping, and then repeating the cycle. The time went much more quickly than I thought it would. It was daylight for awhile but soon the darkness caught up with us again. Because of the International Date Line and the length and direction of our flight, we would land at Mc Chord at virtually the same time we took off from Cam Ranh Bay. I had experienced very few hours of July 26, 1969, because of my trip westbound to Vietnam, but I was making up for that with the longest day of my life on July 22, 1970.

I had just eaten another meal when I heard the engines throttle back and felt the aircraft start its descent. A shiver coursed through my body. I looked out the window into the inky blackness but saw nothing. Over the next few minutes I looked out again and again. Then there it was, a light on the ground. We were no longer over the ocean; we were over Washington. Below me was my home state!

It wasn't long before the glow of lights from Tacoma and maybe Seattle appeared on the northern horizon. I could see the flashing airfield beacon and make out the runway lights at Mc Chord. Lower and lower we descended until I could feel the nose of the aircraft slowly pitch up and then the wheels hit the runway. We were on the ground. I was almost home.

As the airliner taxied off the runway toward the terminal, we again heard from the pilot: "It's my privilege to be the first to welcome you back to the States. You have served your country, and you should be very proud of that. Thank you, and welcome home."

Chapter 49

Comfort, comfort my people,
says your God.
Speak tenderly to Jerusalem,
and cry to her
that her warfare is ended…

--Isaiah 40:1-2a (RSV)

22 July 1970

The cool night dampness of the Pacific Northwest greeted me as I stepped onto the stairway and made my way down. The tropical climate was back there in another part of the globe where I'd left it fifteen hours ago. This felt so much better and smelled so much better. No more acrid smoke from burning human waste. I was almost home.

Into the terminal and of course through some more processing. I glanced at my watch—not quite midnight yet. I'd made it to the States on the twenty-second, two days early.

Most of us changed out of jungle fatigues into our short-sleeved khaki uniforms. Soon we were on buses to Sea-Tac International Airport, less than forty-five minutes away. Lights were everywhere—street lights, vehicle lights, building lights, flood lights, traffic lights, neon lights. I'd forgotten how much a normal city street could be lit up in the US, even after midnight. The arches of a Mc Donald's came into view and could easily have enticed me to stop, but I wasn't in control of the vehicle. I wanted to get home anyway.

Sea-Tac was alive with activity. Guys were buying military stand-by tickets home and were hoping for seats on flights early in the morning. Others didn't want to take the chance of not getting out so they paid more for a reservation and a guaranteed seat. Everyone seemed to be calling home and talking to loved ones—wives, mothers, brothers, you name it. "I'm in the States, and I'll be home in the morning on the first flight out of Seattle," or, "I can get flights out at these times … what works for you to pick me up?" or, "I can't wait to see you, I've missed you so much, I can hardly stand waiting till morning," and a myriad of other conversations.

I found out the local commuter flight to Bellingham left Sea-Tac at 7 a.m. and arrived around 8 a.m. I figured that was the way to go because even if Dad left home now and drove to Seattle to pick me up, I wouldn't get home any earlier. And it probably wasn't a good idea for him or someone else to be doing that much driving in the middle of the night anyway.

I wasn't going to phone home until the sun was coming up, but with everyone else making phone calls the urge was too much to resist. At 2 a.m. I dialed our home phone number in Sumas. After several rings I heard someone pick up: "Hello?" It was my brother Don.

"Hey Don, this is Dale."

"Uh, uh, what? Dale?" It was obvious he wasn't fully awake yet.

"I'm home from Vietnam, I'm in Seattle."

"Uh, you're still in Vietnam?"

"No, I'm in Washington, in Seattle."

"Uh, I can't understand what you're saying," he said haltingly. "Let me get Dad. Oh, here's Dad."

"Hello?" came the voice of Dad.

"Dad, this is Dale. I'm home from Vietnam, I'm in Seattle."

"Oh, Dale. Ah, where are you?" Dad obviously was not fully awake either.

"I'm home from Vietnam and I'm at Sea-Tac airport."

"Oh. You don't want us to come and pick you up now, do you?" He was waking up.

I smiled at that. Ever practical Dad. Yet I knew if I'd indicated that I was hoping they'd jump in the car right now and head to Seattle, he'd probably do so. "No, I'm planning to take the first commuter flight in the morning to Bellingham. It's supposed to arrive there at 8 a.m. If you started driving now, I probably wouldn't get home any earlier."

"Oh, okay. We'll be there to meet you. And we're very thankful that you are home safe and sound." It sounded like his more formal pastor's voice, but I knew he meant it.

"Get some sleep, Dad. I can't wait to see you all."

"We're all looking forward to seeing you, too. Good night, Dale."

There it was, all very logical, all very rational. It was a good common sense decision. But something inside of me craved seeing them in three hours, not six, while it was still dark, something on the spur of the moment, something irrational, something emotional. Oh, well, just a few more hours and I'd be home.

There wasn't much to do the rest of the night. What little conversation we had was rather disconnected and unfocused. The three of us had been pretty much connected at the hip the better part of three days now, so we were essentially talked out. I enjoyed just contemplating my new reality, mulling it over from time to time to make sure it wasn't a dream: I was in the U.S., in my home state, and would be seeing my family in just a few short hours. I would be seeing Donna in a couple weeks, which made me both excited and nervous. Vietnam was truly back there, behind me, more a thing of remembrances and memories, no longer a present reality. I wanted the memories to fade, I didn't want to think about them anymore. I wanted to start the rest of my life.

Every once in awhile my nerves would feel on edge and my muscles would tremble inexplicably. Then I'd get up and walk the mostly empty concourses. A couple times I stepped outside, where the traffic was virtually nonexistent, to smell the sweetness of the night air and perhaps feel some serenity.

Finally the dawn came and it was time to say adios to my friends. I knew I'd be seeing Phil in a few weeks because we both had orders to Fort Benning. But I didn't know when I'd be seeing Dave again.

I bought my ticket to Bellingham, then sat in the gate waiting area by myself for awhile. Soon the flight was called, and I noted I would be the only passenger on it. The pilot led me down a corridor and some steps, and outside onto the tarmac. My final leg home would be in a small, older, dual-engine prop airplane. It didn't take long for the pilot to start his engines and get taxiing clearance. There was very little ground traffic, so we were able to quickly taxi to our runway and take off.

The morning was sunny and clear, one of those spectacular days which makes you glad you are alive and in the Pacific Northwest. As we gained altitude Seattle unfolded below; then Puget Sound and its innumerable islands came into view. A few boats plied the waters, leaving thread-like traces of their passing. Some of the higher Olympic Mountain peaks were almost too brilliant to look at what with the early morning sun reflecting off their snow caps. I imagined that all of western Washington was gifting me with a "welcome home" living postcard.

As we steadily made our way north, Mount Baker, the gem of the north Cascades which dominated the northwest Washington landscape, came into view. If I needed any more assurance I was almost home, that graceful cone-like volcanic creation provided it — this was the same mountain that was framed by our living room picture window. Now it rose majestically before me, draped in a mantle of white, stretching upward into the heavens in praise to its Creator.

I felt a thrill course through my body as the pilot pulled back the throttle and dipped the nose of the aircraft in his initial approach to Bellingham. The minutes of losing altitude, setting flaps, and extending the landing gear in preparation for landing seemed to crawl by interminably. Then, a solid thump, and we were on the ground.

Before we had completed our taxi to the terminal building, I saw clearly my Mom, Dad, and three little brothers—Karl, Ken, and Keith—standing there waiting for the aircraft to arrive. They were flesh and blood with a look of anticipation on their faces. Mom was ready with her camera. No more doubt—I was truly home.

Mom managed to get a picture as I descended the three or four steps of the commuter airplane. A moment later I was in her arms. "It is *so* good to have you home," she said in typical Mom fashion. Yes, it was so good to be home, Mom's teary-eyed face notwithstanding—it always caused a catch in my throat.

"Welcome home, Dale," said Dad in his typically low key, unemotional way. But then we hugged.

The three guys had been growing the past year. "Hi, Dale." "How long ago did you leave Vietnam?" "Was it scary there?"

"Who stretched you guys out?" I responded. They seemed to like the fact that I noticed.

"You boys get with your brother so I can take a picture of you together," Mom directed.

During the thirty-minute ride home to Sumas we chatted about a number of things—home and Vietnam, the weather, how many cuttings of hay the dairy farmers had gotten so far that summer, the baseball standings, our sadness that the Seattle Pilots had moved to Milwaukee and had become the Brewers after only one season in Seattle, and a multitude of other things that reinforced one thing—I was home.

At one point Dad asked, "Did you lose any members of your unit this past year?" I silently nodded my head yes.

Immediately Mom intervened: "Okay, we're not going to talk about that today." *Thanks, Mom.* No way did I want to talk about that. Ever. The boys looked disappointed.

When we pulled into the driveway at home, I could see that little had changed which made me smile. I put my things in the bedroom I shared with my older brother Don, took a long, hot shower, and put on some civvies. I wandered into the kitchen. Mom asked, "Are you hungry, do you want me to make you something to eat?"

"No, I'm not very hungry. I'll just wait till lunch."

Dad was getting some coffee for Mom and him. "Want some coffee?"

"Sounds good."

"Want some chocolate chip cookies?" Mom asked.

"Now you're talking! I'll try not to eat 'em all." I downed about a half dozen with my coffee. Not many things could top the exquisite flavor of a homemade chocolate chip cookie. I just about drooled on my shirt.

Eventually my brothers drifted off to their neighborhood friends, Dad to his study, and Mom to her kitchen and laundry room. A normalcy took over that felt right.

The rest of the day I settled into my room and spent some time wandering through our house, yard, and garden. I walked through the park north of our house and got the mail at the post office while checking out downtown (all three blocks of it!). All seemed to be in order. I would explore further afield the next few days and contact some of my old friends. But today I wanted to hang out at home.

After dinner I continued with my re-Americanization by watching some TV with my little brothers. Don had been home for dinner but had gone out with friends for the evening. It was good to see him again. Dad was in his typical evening spot sitting in his easy chair in the living room, holding a magazine with one hand while tuning in a baseball game on the radio with the other. Mom was near him reading a book. It was how I had imagined it.

I went to bed relatively early. I tried to read a couple pages of a book, but my mind drifted off to other places, to my last few days. Camp Eagle and Sumas seemed to be opposite poles of the earth. They were. And I had been in both places within only a couple days' time. The juxtaposition was too incongruous to wrap my mind around, like they didn't belong in the same world. They didn't. But they were. I was where I wanted to be. It was good. Finally I slipped off to sleep.

KAWUMP! Incoming!

Every muscle and nerve in my body was taut. Something tasted bitter in my throat. Fear and sweat took over my mind and body. I was trying to get under my bed, I didn't dare run to the bunker yet. I kept pulling and pulling. Why wouldn't my mattress come off the bed?

There was a light somewhere. It filled the room. "Dale, what are you doing?" It sounded like my brother's voice, but what would he be doing here?

"Dale, wake up!" Slowly consciousness set in. My brother Don *was* standing there. The room was our bedroom in our home in Sumas. I was lying on the floor with my hands gripping my mattress.

"What happened?" I asked.

"I don't know. You tell me."

"I thought I heard a loud noise."

"Oh, that. After my friend dropped me off, he backed into the trash barrel and mashed it into the tree by the driveway."

"Did it sound kinda like a 'kawump,' kinda like two syllables?"

"Yeah, I guess you could say that. He hit the garbage can and then it hit the tree."

"I guess it sounded like incoming."

"What were you trying to do?"

"I always got down on the floor and pulled my mattress over me till I thought it was safe to run to the bunker."

"You must not have had a big mattress with innersprings."

"No."

"You gonna be okay?"

My fingers finally uncurled from the edges of my mattress, and I realized they'd been tightly clenched this whole time. "Yeah, I think I'll be fine."

"I'm gonna brush my teeth and get ready for bed."

"Please turn out the light."

Now I was lying awake again in the dark trying to think through what had just happened. My sheets felt clammy from my sweat. I realized I was in Sumas, but I couldn't get away from Vietnam. *Am I going to have to keep thinking and worrying about that stuff even here? I came home to get away from that. Oh, man, I don't even want any part of that. What if it's the middle of the day on some street corner and some noise sets me off? People will think I'm crazy. I've got to figure out how to turn off my mind to the past year. I want Vietnam to be gone.*

As I lay there in the dark stillness, my thoughts wandered around, exploring the situation from different angles. *But there were some good things that happened there, too. You did your job, for the most part. ...Yeah, but you can't have the good only, because the crap will be right there with it. Why can't I just forget about it, like I was never there? Sumas is so different from Camp Eagle. Since I'm in Sumas, why can't I just think about what's happening here?*

I lay there awhile, letting this idea sink in.

I am home. I have to remember that. This is my new reality. I guess it'll be awhile before I can forget the past, if ever. But that's not what's happening to me now. Mom and Dad and my brothers are in the same house I'm in. I said goodnight to them. And when I wake up in the morning they'll still be here. I'll see my sisters before the summer is over. This is where many of my friends are. And I'll see my church family on Sunday. All these people are real. They know me and I know them. They'll probably even be glad to see me. And in a couple weeks I'll be going to Michigan to meet a beautiful young lady again. Yeah, I'm nervous about that. But I have to at least give it a try. She's just too special not to... Okay, Petersen, you gotta remember: you are home now, and you've got the rest of your life ahead of you. ... Thank you, Lord.

EPILOGUE

More than thirty-seven years have passed since the day of my homecoming in July 1970. Like much of my past history, I was never able to forget about it. In retrospect, I would not have wanted to do so. That year in Vietnam is as much a part of who I am as are any of my other experiences. That is not to say that some of my reflections and remembrances over the years have not been difficult, even painful. They have. But wrestling with the difficult can have a positive effect on spiritual and character development, among other things.

For several years after my return to the States I struggled with the fundamental question of whether the war was right or wrong. By that I mean the overall reasons and objectives which were the genesis of the war, not the war strategy and its implementation. Of course it's often not easy to separate the two, but I think it's important to try to do so. If the original reasons and objectives were noble and meant to have a positive purpose for those affected by the war, the war strategy to meet those objectives could still be flawed—and therefore "wrong"—or the strategy could be effective. However, if the original premise was morally bankrupt, then the war strategy will suffer the same condemnation.

In my younger years I got caught up in the arguments of the anti-war movement. I was sure they had the answer—the war was morally wrong and therefore everything that flowed from it was evil. That included me and my participation in it. But over time, the more I thought about it, I wasn't so sure anymore. I found myself moving toward the opposite conclusion. Suffice it to say that in recent years I have been able finally to arrive at the conclusion that it was honorable for me to answer the call of my country when it came to Vietnam.

What about Donna? Well, I did make that trip to Michigan in August 1970. She met me at the Detroit airport, and my first thought was that she was more beautiful than I had remembered. By the time we had driven the forty-five minutes to her parents' home, I had lost my nervousness and felt relaxed and at ease. I felt like I already knew her quite well from her letters. During those two weeks we had together I got to know her in ways I couldn't through letters: how she talked, her non-verbal communications, what her smiles were like and what elicited them, what it was like to look into her eyes, and, yes, what it was like to hold her closely and feel the softness of her skin (and that's as far as I'll go with that subject!). It didn't take long for me to realize I was madly in love with her, and she with me.

At the end of August my leave was over and I had to report to Fort Benning, Georgia. From that time forward I would go to Michigan, every three weeks or so, to spend a long weekend with her. We became engaged on Valentine's Day, 1971, and were married June 12, 1971.

We are still happily (most of the time!) married thirty-six plus years later.

By the time we were married, I was out of the Army. Originally I was supposed to stay in the Army until May 1972. But at the beginning of 1971, the Army announced an "early out" for helicopter pilots who'd already had an overseas tour—apparently there was a glut of helicopter pilots because of cuts in troop strength in Vietnam. We had a choice of getting out on 1 April 1971, or we could go "voluntary indefinite" which could mean another tour in Vietnam. For me the choice was easily made. That also marked the end of my flying days.

Three days after we were married I started college classes again. This time I stuck with it and graduated two years later from Calvin College in Grand Rapids, Michigan.

I got to see the movie "Butch Cassidy and the Sundance Kid" in its entirety in August 1971 in Grand Rapids.

I smoked my last cigarette on March 21, 1974. Our first child was born in August 1974. Yes, the two events are connected.

What about my relationship with God? I believe I have grown in that relationship over my adult years. That is not to say I haven't struggled at times with doubt, with drifting away from him, with being so consumed with myself and my own thing that I didn't have time for him.

But if there's anything I have learned from God over the years, this is of central importance:

> *This I recall to my mind, therefore I have hope.*
> *The Lord's lovingkindnesses indeed never cease,*
> *For His compassions never fail.*
> *They are new every morning;*
> *Great is Thy faithfulness.*
> --Lamentations 3:21-23 (NASB)

God's greatest lovingkindness to me is the gift of his son Jesus. The same God who "...knit me together in my mother's womb" (Psalm 139:13 NIV) is the God who gave me new birth through his Son. Jesus took my place by shedding his blood and dying on the cross for my sins. God forgave my sins and gave me eternal life because of what Jesus did. It is by grace he did this; it is nothing I could ever do or earn myself. In addition, he made me his son by adopting me into his family. Because of this, he is my Father. In Vietnam he was always with me, walking with me, carrying me, giving me what I needed for each day — so often when I didn't even realize it. He allowed me to question him, to doubt him, to be angry with him. And he comforted me and gave me his peace when I had none.

As my Father, he has my best interests at heart. In fact, he works out all things, good or bad, whether I understand it or not, for my good. I don't know why Vietnam happened. I don't know why I lost good friends there or why I was spared. It is something that still makes me very sad at times. But I know he had a good reason for bringing me home safely and keeping me here on earth all these years after Vietnam. It is part of his good and gracious plan for me. I know I will die some day, maybe tomorrow, maybe thirty years from now. When I do, it will be by his plan, and I will be in his presence for eternity.

God's lovingkindnesses, great and small, have been innumerable in my life. Here are just a few: He gave me loving and selfless parents—one of their greatest goals was that my siblings and I would truly know God and his Word, and would make that central to who we are. And he gave me loving and caring siblings who have done just that.

In Donna, God gifted me with my wife, my companion, my confidant, my lover, my friend. I simply could not have been the person I am without her walking alongside me.

Three mornings rise up above the rest in Donna's and my married life together. They are August 13, 1974; September 16, 1976; and June 28, 1980. On those dates we experienced the births of Amie, Nathan, and Melissa. I thrilled to the sight of their miraculous first breaths. Since then they have given my life incredible joy, meaning, and fullness.

God continues with his lovingkindnesses to me: he has given me my awesome sons- and daughter-in-law: Matt, Michelle, and Mark, who have deep and abiding love for my children. And now I have grandchildren — Ian, Jadon, Julia, and Eva — and perhaps others still to come. Those little tykes are so precious to me.

Throughout all my life God has been faithful to me — not because he had to, but because of his overwhelming love and grace. Ultimately my life is not about me, it's about God and his kingdom, his will. And it is to him I give the glory.

GLOSSARY

101st: 101st Airborne Division (Airmobile)

AC: aircraft commander

AFVN: Armed Forces Vietnam Network

AH-1G Cobra: a helicopter gunship, normally outfitted with a 7.62-mm mini-gun and 2.75-inch folding fin rockets

AGB: accessory gearbox—drives two generators, three hydraulic pumps, one oil pump, and one hydraulic motor pump; operated by the auxiliary power unit until main engines are on line

AGL: above ground-level

AO: area of operation.

APU: auxiliary power unit—a small sixty-horsepower turbine engine which provides hydraulic pressure to drive the main engine starter motors

ARVN: Army of the Republic of Viet Nam

ASHB: Assault Support Helicopter Battalion, a CH-47 Chinook battalion.

arty: artillery

BX: base exchange—essentially the same as a PX, but located on an Air Force Base.

beep: engine beep trim switch

337

bush: the field, the jungle, the boonies, anywhere on the ground outside a camp perimeter

C-130: a US Air Force four-engine, propeller-driven cargo airplane

C-rations: Combat rations — three or four cans of food, with a pack of four cigarettes, all in a small cardboard box

CH-47 Chinook: a tandem-rotor, twin engine heavy-lift cargo helicopter

CO: commanding officer

CP: command post

CWO: Chief Warrant Officer — a higher ranking warrant officer

cannon cocker: artillery personnel

Charlie, Charlie Cong: Viet Cong or NVA soldier

chicken plate: armored chest protector

Chuck: variant of "Charlie"

comm.: radio communications

cowboying: Flying an aircraft at close to its operational limits, sometimes recklessly or with less than full regard for recognized safe operating procedures

cyclic stick: controls the tilt of the rotor plane and therefore the direction and speed of the helicopter

DEROS: date of estimated return from overseas

DMZ: de-militarized zone separating North from South Vietnam

dee-dee or dee-dee mau: get out of here quickly

density altitude: a function of pressure altitude and temperature—the higher that either component is, the higher the density altitude. The higher the density altitude, the less lift for an aircraft.

donut: a circular piece of thick fabric which connects a cargo net and sling to the cargo hook on a Chinook to carry an external load

Dust-off: medical evacuation (or medivac) helicopter, usually a Huey

engine beep trim switch: switch that controls the power settings of the Chinook's engines—something like the accelerator in a car—and therefore the rotor RPM

Freedom Bird: airliner which brings a soldier back home to the States after his Vietnam tour is completed

gooks: disparaging term for VC or NVA soldiers

grunts: infantrymen

Guard: an emergency radio frequency monitored by all aircraft. It was used for Mayday calls as well as safety critical messages.

HQ: headquarters

hootch: living quarters

IFR: Instrument Flight Rules — rules or procedures used for flying when one needs to fly by his instruments because he does not have any reference to the ground, usually because his aircraft is in the clouds. The opposite of IFR is VFR, or visual flight rules.

Indian country: slang for enemy territory

KIA: killed in action

knot: nautical mile per hour, or nautical mile (one knot = 1.15 "statute" or "normal" miles per hour)

LOH-6: Light Observation Helicopter, or Loach, used primarily as an airborne scout, but also could be outfitted with weapons and used as a small gunship

LRRP: long-range reconnaissance patrol

LZ: landing zone

MPC: military payment certificates — used in place of greenback dollars in Vietnam

nI: the nI indicator is a tachometer which displays turbine speed in percentages